THE ULTIMATE HUNT

JIM GRASSI

Jim Grassi

Matt. 4:19

HARVEST HOUSE PUBLISHERS
Eugene, Oregon 97402

Cover photo courtesy of John Sax, Tree Tops, Rotorua, New Zealand

Cover by Left Coast Design, Portland, Oregon

THE ULTIMATE HUNT
Copyright © 2000 by Jim Grassi
Published by Harvest House Publishers
Eugene, Oregon 97402

Library of Congress Cataloging-in-Publication Data

Grassi, James E., 1943-
    The ultimate hunt/Jim Grassi.
        p. cm.
    ISBN: 1-56507-950-7
    1. Hunting—Religious aspects—Christianity. I. Title

BV4597.4.G735 2000
242'.68—dc21

00-024150

Printed in the United States of America.

00 01 02 03 04 05 06 07 08 09 / BP-BG / 10 9 8 7 6 5 4 3 2 1

Contents

Acknowledgments

In speaking about gratitude, the esteemed Reverend Willis P. King said, "Gratitude is from the same root word as 'grace,' which signifies the free and boundless mercy of God. Thanksgiving is from the same root as 'think,' so that to think is to thank."

I'm extremely grateful to A. W. Tozer and his wonderful teachings on the character of God. It is obvious that Tozer's walk with God was a high priority with him and he allowed nothing to interfere. His scholarly efforts have enabled me to continue climbing toward a spiritual horizon that will no doubt affect my life and future works.

This project could not have been possible without the constant love, support and understanding of my wonderful bride of thirty-five years. Thank you, Louise, for being my faithful partner. It is a real blessing to work together for God's kingdom.

I'm especially indebted to all my ministry partners, supporters and board members who have faithfully served with our twenty-year Let's Go Fishing Ministry. At the beginning of this work my longtime friend and co-worker, Gary Chase, lost his fight with cancer and went to be with the Lord. Later in the project, my friend and pastor, Bruce Miles, also became critically ill and died. Their Christ-like lives were a tremendous inspiration how we should apply the traits of God to our lives.

Both Dr. Karen Hayter and Ronna Snyder are special friends who also provided enormous encouragement to this weary hunter.

As any author will tell you, the stress and strain attributed to enduring the twelve-hour days of sitting in one place without much exercise can create many problems with a "bad back." I count it a blessing to have a good physical therapist and chiropractor who have enabled me to endure those long, hard days at the computer. Thank you, Kimberlee Hammond of Dynamic Rehab and Dr. Bruce Grandstaff.

Finally, I once again commend and thank the very gifted staff at Harvest House Publishers. Their amazing talents and enthusiasm have encouraged me to perfect and refine the concepts involved in this difficult work.

Thank you—Jesus!

"Grow in the grace and knowledge of the Lord and Savior Jesus Christ" (2 Peter 3:18).

*Dedicated to future generations of sportsmen and women
who enjoy God's Great Outdoors,
especially my wonderful grandchildren:*

*Madeline Louise Grassi
Tyler Thomas Grassi
Dana Rose Grassi*

May you know the true character of God.

A Note from the Author

As we prepare to move into the twenty-first century, our high-tech culture continues to struggle with its identity. People seek lasting values, moral integrity and good memories that are rarely experienced in a high-pressure environment.

The sheer expansion of urbanization has taken away many of the quiet open spaces where man could spend time contemplating life and communicating with the Creator. Decades ago many folks could simply open their back doors and seek out a place of solitude. Those seeking to really explore nature must now make an effort to find remote areas often hours from the congested communities in which they live.

A mixture of feelings can be experienced in the great outdoors. Joy, fear, excitement, apprehension, wonder, exhilaration and fascination are just some of the emotions that one can benefit from while pursuing wilderness activities. When we encounter these feelings, there are numerous opportunities to interact with God's creation while evaluating our personal strengths and weaknesses.

A good hunter learns to adapt, to fit, and to flow with the situation. Snowstorms or a shroud of fog may cause the hunter to modify his planned stalk to the top of the mountain where he knows a trophy buck hides. It is through these experiences that we learn of God's patience and dominion.

For some, being an outdoorsman is like connecting with our primitive side. We have innate curiosities about the unknown that God placed in our spirit. Some would say that men are basically hunters and gatherers by nature and need the outdoor experience to satisfy their longings. Maybe it is the excitement of being a kid again. Dressing up for the adventure and preparing oneself for the challenge produces a youthful response among many outdoorsmen.

The Ultimate Hunt is a book about outdoor adventure and life-changing decisions that affect our knowledge of, and behavior toward God. After surveying racks of Christian books, I've discovered very little written about knowing God's character. If we are to experience His likeness, we need to know and understand His basic nature. The more we identify with His character, the more God can imprint His likeness upon our lives. When we discover His character, we can better understand what makes God God.

By sharing some of my favorite hunting stories and the testimonies of renowned outdoorsmen, I hope to inspire and motivate our thinking about what it means to know God and make Him known.

When Jesus selected men to represent His kingdom, He chose eight sportsmen (fishermen) to be among His elite group of disciples. The "Master's Men" were real guys who weren't caught up in worshiping stained-glass windows, idols, or ceremonies. They were guys with failures and challenges who directed their passions to becoming real hunters and fishers of men's souls. In a similar manner, the prominent men portrayed in this work seek to use their outdoor skills to reach others with the Good News that impacts our destiny.

The goal of this work is to take practical adventures from everyday life and tie them to eternal meanings, especially as they relate to the character of God. Through the use of metaphors, anecdotes, parables, analogies, and even some humor, I wish to encourage readers to become stronger in their faith and get better acquainted with God's great outdoors.

Prominently displayed on the wall of a room in our home is the following verse: "The steps of a good man are ordered by the LORD, and he delighteth in his way. Though fall, shall not be utterly cast down: for the Lord upholdeth him with His hand" (Psalm 37:23, 24 KJV). If we are to be in His hand we must be in His continual presence. And being in His continual presence we will be in His sight, ready to take aim on THE ULTIMATE HUNT in life—knowing God!

A prepared hunter will fill his pack with a variety of items that help make his trip safer, more comfortable and efficient in harvesting his quarry. Every item will be carefully chosen for its benefit and function. Anything that is useless or burdensome just gets in the way and weighs down the determined hunter.

Some reading this book will find that their packs (lives) are overfilled with feelings of loneliness, fear, temptation, rejection, anxiousness, or despair. God intended for us to so understand His character that we would fill our packs with His grace, mercy, forgiveness, love, peace, comfort, joy, goodness, sufficiency, power, and tenderness.

I pray that this reading will help all of us to evaluate our spiritual packs so that we can live a more productive, joy-filled life. God wants to be our trail companion and is willing to share the burden by toting our over-burdened packs.

When you are lost in the woods of life, when your pathways of decisions are overgrown with thorny bushes, when all your earthly trails are uphill struggles, or when it seems there are few answers from a God who seems removed, take comfort, my friend. Know that God has your heart in His sight and that He wishes for you to pursue Him.

Through the words of this book and the meditations of your heart, may you embrace the help and encouragement that the greatest Hunter of all can provide. God has been hunting for men's hearts since He introduced His great creation to Adam and Eve.

So let's sight in our bows, sling our guns and pack our bags for *The Ultimate Hunt.*

First Shot

Since the beginning of creation, man has been fascinated with the sport of hunting. Participating in this activity allows us to view the majesty of God's great outdoors from the front-line. Through absorbing the beauty that every sunrise and sunset bring, exploring the grandeur of each mountainside, appreciating the isolated pockets of wildflowers on a picturesque meadow, or experiencing the backdrop of a quiet pond, we can enjoy special moments of pleasure with the wild members of creation. For those who frequent the woods and plains seeking to match their wits and skills against their quarry, one can know the magnetic pull and attraction that help us explore in detail the creative habits and habitats of each critter.

People who love the outdoors willingly endure days in the field for the sake of challenging, protecting, and enjoying the creatures that are ultimately used for sustenance, clothing, or memory-building anecdotes. The stories and events contained in this work are true. Each chapter contributes to our understanding of hunting and knowing the character of God. Through the experiences and professional hunting techniques of renowned hunters, outdoor photographers, professional athletes, friends, and pastors, you will learn new hunting strategies while better understanding the nature of God and His desire to have fellowship with mankind.

This book is for dedicated hunters, photographers or aspiring hunters who wish to more fully experience the presence of God in their lives while improving upon their outdoor skills.

Chapter 1

Knowing God Through Creation

God the Creator

It is rare in today's machismo environment to find a person who places enjoyment of the hunting experience over the taking of the game. My friend Pastor John Morgan is one such man. Not only is he one of the nation's top pastors, who every Sunday welcomes more than 12,000 members to his Houston, Texas, church; he also is considered one of the top hunters in the United States.

Taking a tour of his office and home, you might conclude that he shoots everything he sees. On the contrary, this international hunter is a strong advocate for game management programs that have helped propagate a variety of species around the world.

In 1998 John joined a group of other evangelists I had assembled to help ignite a revival in New Zealand. After our conference, I invited John and his wife to visit one of the infamous "fair-chase" red stag game preserves. Despite some inclement weather, John and his hunting partner, Johnnie Lowe, stalked and photographed a number of marvelous animals that would have made the Safari Club record book.

On the first day, Pastor John saw a nice big stag that he graciously allowed his partner to take. The adrenaline was flowing as they anticipated the next day's hunt for John's stag.

The next morning came with more inclement weather—and it was only a few hours before John and his wife would have to depart for their next speaking engagement in Africa. As they left the lodge, the guide suggested that the two hunters move to a new location and look at some different animals.

As they strolled along a ridge, John spotted an awesome stag that would have scored well in the record book. It was everything John wanted in his first stag. In order to avoid detection, the group slowly crawled to an area that provided some bush cover that would help separate them from the unsuspecting animal.

As they peered through the scrub brush, they could see the large head and neck of the older stag that was framed by eighteen beautiful ivory white points. The group continued to study the animal until, just as the guide predicted, the deer moved out of the cover to gather in some warmth from the sun breaking between the dark cloud cover.

The guide handed John a borrowed rifle with the warning that it had been difficult to sight in this gun. "The rifle doesn't seem to properly group the shots. We can't figure it out. Maybe the scope is not mounted correctly," the guide said. John peered through the scope and sighted in on the perfect shot just behind the shoulder bone.

John recalls: "I studied the stag for several minutes knowing that I could take him at any time. The animal was totally unaware of the imminent danger and lingered in the sunlight with his head proudly held high." John to this day is reminded of that perfect moment and awesome responsibility he had when the majestic animal turned sideways. "Whenever I hunt I'm mindful of the tremendous privilege and responsibility it is to take the life of a game animal."

As John's finger tightened up on the trigger slack, he felt the call to re-evaluate his decision. "I felt uneasy about taking a shot with a gun that may not be totally accurate. Also, knowing that we only had a couple of hours before I had to leave, I was convinced that it did not allow me the time to properly enjoy the unique experience and spiritual adventure which occurs after the smoke clears away."

The guide and operator are still talking about the patience and discipline John demonstrated in respecting God's creation and timing. They can't believe that he would not chance an errant shot to gain the bragging rights to that awesome deer. John's philosophy is simple, "God usually rewards me at a later date or in a different way if I respect His creation and observe good judgment in my hunting experiences."

What would have been your response? Are you able to see beyond the immediate reward to appreciating the beauty of the creation?

A Special Kind of Outdoorsman

John says he feels particularly close to God when he is hunting or fishing. He regularly reminds himself of the promises shared in Scripture, "For since the creation of the world God's invisible qualities—his eternal power and divine nature—have been clearly seen, being understood from what has been made, so that men are without excuse" (Romans 1:20).

Most hunters know that many wonderful traits of our Creator can be seen in nature. Special sportsmen like Pastor John Morgan see beyond the experience to the wonder of creation. They see God's handiwork and are constantly amazed as to the craftsmanship that our Creator has used to design the proper setting for each animal. "You don't find a majestic red stag in an Arizona desert; or a duck landing on a cactus; or a coyote on top of an alpine mountain," John says. "You find each animal in a unique environment that is perfectly designed for his or her characteristics and nature. It is as if God not only drew the picture but placed the perfect frame around each creation."

It was not easy for John to ease up on that trigger in New Zealand. His respect for God's power over creation and his ethical approach to hunting allowed him to anticipate that God may again give him a chance to properly stalk a trophy stag. John walked away from his New Zealand stag with a smile on his face and an old gospel song in his heart: "Count your blessings, name them one by one. Count your blessings, see what God has done."

Are We Good Stewards of God's Creation?

In my writing and personal life I try to bridge the gap between those who enjoy the outdoors and urbanites. I respect those who feel that hunting has the appearance of being a barbaric ritual that has no relevant place in modern civilization. The fact remains that almost 20 million Americans still consider this outdoor activity an enriching experience that helps shape a person's character while providing sustenance and recreation.

Some enjoy the challenge of the elements and conquering fearful situations. Still others believe the wilderness provides unique and intimate fellowship opportunities that can only come from sharing a day in the woods and an evening campfire. To almost everyone it is a chance to encounter the Creator in His backyard.

I have a deep love for all God has created. His divine plan provided for an awesome creation; however, the only thing He created with a soul was man. He gave man dominion over all His creation so that he might enjoy and use it to sustain life. Scripture suggests that in God's plan animals had a purpose of sacrifice, food, clothing and recreation.

It is helpful to remember that God did not put animals on the earth for us to worship. His Son died on the cross for man not wild animals. God also demands that we be good stewards of His resources and properly respect their value. To do this He provided laws of order to guide man in his approach to managing nature.

Without some controlled hunting we would not be able to sustain a healthy population of wildlife. Overcrowding and disease would soon settle in on the wild and domestic animal populations, threatening the balance God intended. We should hunt not to brag or boast, not to wastefully slaughter game, nor to destroy or devour for selfish gain. Outdoorsmen must respect God's creation as they carefully and selectively take animals that are in abundance.

A balance in nature comes when man acknowledges the power of God over His creation. Ask most hunters to define power and you will most likely receive a short list of descriptive phrases such as 300 Winchester magnum, 90-pound dual-cam compound bow, 50-power spotting scope or 500-pound angry mother bear. These manifestations of power all have their limitations.

The power of God is matchless in its scope and magnitude. The power to create the far-reaching heavens while caring enough to tend for the needs of a hummingbird is beyond our comprehension.

The Power of God over Creation

God's awesome power is manifested in many ways. Certainly one of the more visible displays of His magnificence is the diversity of His creation. As the prophet Isaiah reminds us, "Lift your eyes and look to the heavens: Who created all these? He who brings out the starry hosts one by one, and calls them each by name. Because of his great power and mighty strength, not one of them is missing" (Isaiah 40:26).

The Bible reminds us that God created all things and it was good. From the beginning He gave man dominion over the animals. God placed man in a permanent position over His creation and challenged him to enjoy, manage and properly utilize wildlife.

God's imagination and sensitivity defined a diverse and complex animal kingdom. One way to verify the existence of a Supreme Being is to analyze what He creates. We can find some of the character of God by studying His works. His personality, His wonder, His magnificence and His traits are exemplified with every atom and molecule that forms life. The intricacies and beauty that form our natural resources are stunning.

"The scientist who collects and catalogs and the child who wanders barefoot through the woods are equally awestruck by the sheer profusion of creatures that populate this planet," Tozer writes. "The child marvels at the psychedelic design of a butterfly; he chases darting 'skeeter hawks' (dragonflies), yelps at the spastic leap of a click beetle, or breathlessly fondles a baby rabbit. The scientist looks closer. He takes a simple block of forest soil, one-foot square and one inch deep, and begins counting. In this loamy world that we so thoughtlessly tread upon he finds 'an average of 1,356 living creatures, including 865 mites, 265 springtails, 22 millipedes, 19 adult beetles, and various numbers of 12 other forms' "[1]

When you see geese flying along in "V" formation, you might consider what science has discovered about the wonder of God's creation as to why they fly that way. As each bird flaps its wings, it creates uplift for the bird immediately following. By flying in "V" formation, the whole flock has at least a 71 percent greater flying range than if each bird flew on its own. In a similar manner, people who share a common direction and a sense of community can get where they are going more quickly and easily because they are traveling on the thrust of one another. When a goose falls out of formation, it suddenly feels the drag and resistance of trying to go it alone—and quickly gets back into formation to take advantage of the lifting power of the bird in front. If we have as much sense as a goose, we will stay in formation with those people who are headed the same way we are.

When the head goose gets tired, it rotates back in the wing and another goose flies point. It is sensible to take turns doing demanding jobs, whether with people or with geese flying south. Geese honk from behind to encourage those up front to keep up their speed. What messages do we give when we honk from behind?

Finally—and this is important—when a goose gets sick or is wounded by gunshot, and falls out of formation, two other geese fall out with that goose and follow it down to lend help and protection. They stay with the fallen goose until it is able to fly or until it dies, and only then do they launch out on their own, or with another formation to catch up with their group. If we have the sense God gave a goose, we will stand by each other in a similar manner.

Does God Care About His Creation?

God's creation is fearfully and wonderfully made. God's word tells us that He demonstrates His power and care for creation. The "God-Man," Jesus, reminds us: "Are not five sparrows sold for two pennies? Yet not one of them is forgotten by God" (Luke 12:6). In His infinite wisdom He elected to partner with mankind in utilizing these resources. From early on God gave man permission to use game in ceremony as sacrifices for worship (Exodus 20:24; Leviticus 1:5), for clothing (Genesis 3:21), material for the Tabernacle (Exodus 25:5; 26:14), food supply (Genesis 9:3), instruments of divine providence (Jonah 1, 2, 4), and prophetic fulfillment (1 Kings 21:17-19; 22:37,38).

God encouraged man to enjoy and use these creatures for our benefit and sustenance. Despite all the compassionate rhetoric of animal-rights activists, God has not retracted His original authorization found in Genesis 9 which allows for man to hunt and consume game.

If God has the power over His creation, then He certainly has the right to determine how the fish and game should be utilized. His permissive will and direct instructions suggest that the taking of game is necessary and appropriate.

Get Permission from the Owner

God has shared His power over creation with man. Appreciating God's creation implies stewardship. Without stewardship we have chaos. Even during Old Testament times there was a sense of responsibility and control. For the survival of the species, God has trusted man with good game management practices. To protect His creation He asked Noah to carefully control the numbers and species associated with loading the ark. The carrying capacity of the ark was finite, as is the environment in which we hunt. The control man has over game allows us to properly respect the creation and Creator.

Who has provided permission for man to become a hunter? Permission that hunting is an acceptable activity was provided by the Creator and recorded for posterity in several Bible stories. More than four thousand years ago, God found a man named Nimrod who appeared on the stage of history. While we really don't know a lot about this character, God's inspired word tells us, "He was a mighty hunter before the LORD; that is why it is said, 'Like Nimrod, a mighty hunter before the LORD'" (Genesis 10:9).

In that same book we see that Esau was described as a "skillful hunter" (Genesis 25:27). Despite Esau's immoral and godless life, God granted him and others the privilege of taking the life of an animal for human sustenance (see Genesis 9:1-5).

The direct voice of God can be traced back to a conversation with Noah: "Everything that lives and moves will be food for you. Just as I gave you the green plants, I now give you everything [referring to the animals]" (Genesis 9:3).

To further illustrate His support of such practice, God gave specific directions on the preparation of game for consumption: "But you must not eat meat that has its lifeblood still in it. And for your lifeblood I will surely demand an accounting. I will demand an accounting from every animal. And from each man, too, I will demand an accounting for the life of his fellow man" (Genesis 9:4, 5).

Not only is it okay to hunt; it is also permissible to enjoy and eat this game as expressed in Deuteronomy 14:5. The deer, the gazelle, the toe deer, the wild goat, the ibex, the antelope and the mountain sheep were on King Solomon's menu.

Certainly Jesus regularly directed His fishermen disciples to their bounty. He told Peter to "catch a fish that had a silver coin in its mouth." On two other occasions Jesus directed His disciples to cast their nets into the Sea of Galilee to catch an abundance of fish (see Luke 5 and John 21). In each adventure Jesus directed the action, and I'm sure He celebrated with the disciples as they enjoyed the harvest.

With Permission Comes Responsibility

The book of Genesis tells us that God preserved the animals and birds from the great flood by directing them to Noah's ark (see Genesis 6-9). His power over creation reaches into the very spirit of the animals. God's sensitivity again is manifested in Christ as He told His disciples, "Are not five sparrows sold for two pennies? Yet not one of them is forgotten by God" (Luke 12:6). He cares for His creation. His power and authority over it define His love.

As much as He cares for the birds of the air and the fish of the sea, He has a greater care for you and me. God's directives on managing and being responsible for His creation could not be made any clearer than in Proverbs 12:10:"A righteous man cares for the needs of his animal, but the kindest acts of the wicked are cruel." Being a compassionate and responsible hunter honors the power of God.

To be responsible we must be sensitive to appropriate restrictions on our behavior and attitudes regarding the harvesting of game. Our God is orderly and intentional about obeying His commands and the "rule of order" in the land in which we live. Certainly the apostle Paul's encouragement to the Christians in Rome is relevant today. We need to submit ourselves to governing authorities (Romans 13:1-7). We can respect the power of the Creator over His creation by applying sound game management practices and conservation to help propagate the species. God has entrusted His creation to our stewardship.

I'm very proud of the conservation programs instituted by many of the national associations. Our elk, deer, turkey, duck and buffalo populations are being sustained and even enhanced because membership organizations have taken proactive strategies that enhance our environment and promote the propagation of healthy game populations.

Countless national organizations and local clubs work cooperatively with state and federal resource agencies in habitat improvement, land and water reclamation projects, restocking programs and propagation programs that significantly enhance the opportunities to effectively manage the species. This is honoring the Creator and His power to rule over the land.

Can I Be a Christian and a Hunter?

Dr. Tom C. Rakow, president of the Christian Deer Hunters Association, has an extensive work on this topic. In his excellent booklet titled "Hunting and the Bible," he introduces hunter-author Elmer Smick, who writes in his dictionary: "The Christian must find an answer that centers around God's purpose in putting animals on the earth. God's command that Adam and Eve multiply and subdue the earth (Genesis 1:28) was not an invitation to destroy nature."

Indeed, the biblical definition of dominion involves both accountability and responsibility. Throughout the Old Testament when the chosen people of God met to worship, they were instructed by God to offer a blood sacrifice to the Lord upon their altars. Animals were clearly distinct from man, as Christ came to save mankind and not the other created beings.

Smick clarifies the relationship that exists between humans and other creatures by stating that it was God who "subordinated the animals to man and gave man a responsibility toward them which was similar to God's relationship to us. That responsibility was to care for them, as God cared. But as glory in the context of his good and holy nature, so may man use the animals, but with responsibility."[2]

We are distinct because we are made "in the image of God" (Genesis 1:27). Pastor John Morgan reminds us, "Man is a living soul. Jesus died on the cross for man. He did not die on the cross for animals. And from the beginning of time, God gave man dominion over the animals. God has demanded that we be good stewards of His resources and wildlife management."

Most of the sportsmen I know agree that there needs to be a high level of accountability. One warden suggested, "When it comes right down to it, what you do in the field is between you and God." We respect the power and might of God by honoring His creation. Remember that we should worship the Creator, not the creation. Nature is ours to enjoy and protect.

God's power and presence are to be respected. He has carefully and completely packaged the beautiful gift of creation that we enjoy. Let's do our part in preserving, protecting and carefully utilizing this awesome wonder. Like the prophet Nehemiah, let's remember to worship and praise God for the wonder of His creation. "You alone are the LORD. You made the heavens, even the highest heavens, and all their starry host, the earth and all that is on it, the seas and all that is in them. You give life to everything, and the multitudes of heaven worship you" (Nehemiah 9:6).

Personal Application

- Can you see how God is the Father of all creation? What does that mean to you?

  Read Romans 1:20 and Genesis 1

- How does God care about His creation? How do you feel He cares about you?

  Read Luke 12:6

- What is our responsibility to God and His creation?

  Read Proverbs 12:6

- God's greatest desire for us is that we seek diligently to know Him. What does this verse mean to you: "The fear of the Lord is the beginning of wisdom, and the knowledge of the Holy One is understanding" (Proverbs 9:10).

Chapter 2

Memories of Monarchs

God Jehovah

On a trip to Nashville, Tennessee, with my musically talented twin sons, we had an appointment to meet with recording artist-songwriter Paul Overstreet. While interviewing Paul for a chapter in my second book *Heaven on Earth*, we discussed our common passion for the great outdoors.

Knowing of his passion for hunting, I queried, "Bagged any game lately?"

Paul's frown and slumped shoulders told it all. His busy recording schedule allowed him only a few precious opportunities to stalk game in his home state. "Unfortunately, there has been plenty hiking but very little shooting. The game is scarce and the hunters plentiful," Paul lamented. I could identify with his frustration and disappointment because my experience was no better.

There was no doubt about Paul's enthusiasm for the hunt, so I invited him to view a new hunting video I had produced on some private red stag hunting properties in New Zealand. I asked Paul if he had a good heart that could handle the adrenaline rush that would come from viewing such a video.

Paul looked at me with a puzzled stare and said, "Are the animals in New Zealand really that awesome?"

A few weeks later I asked Paul how he had enjoyed the video. He was hyperventilating with excitement. His manager later told me, "When Paul saw the video his eyes bugged out like a raccoon seeing a platter full of fried fish." Recognizing Paul's excitement, I asked, "Well, what do you think?"

Paul bellowed out, "When do we go? I have never seen trophy game like that anywhere!"

Within a few months I had put together a group of Christian leaders to accompany me to the Land Down Under for a discipleship conference. My good kiwi (New Zealander) friends and entrepreneurs, John and Alma Sax, had arranged to have a couple of hundred South Pacific pastors and lay leaders at the conference to hear our group discuss a variety of church-related topics.

The video and a few brochures describing the world-class red stag taken off John's Rotorua property (Tree Tops) the year before caused all of us to dream about the possibility of shooting one of the progeny from these great deer. Reviewing many of the New Zealand historical game books, I noticed that the genetics of the Rotorua herd had produced some of the top stags ever recorded.

Tree Tops is a semi-fair chase property with two sides of the land heavily fenced to keep out poachers and uninvited guests. The combination of controlled access, a few imported genetically superior studs and good game management practices has developed this property into one of the best trophy stag hunting areas in the world.

Excitement was in the air as we touched down at Auckland Airport. Our conference was well received and allowed a little time for Paul and me to get some archery practice on the large lawn area next to John and Alma's gracious estate in Auckland. My sights were still properly aligned, and we had no problem hitting targets at forty and fifty yards.

After the conference, we wheeled our way about two hours south to the cultural center of New Zealand—Rotorua. The kiwi charm and great hospitality I had experienced in my seven previous New Zealand trips was once again demonstrated.

After a short hike through part of the hunting preserve, we spotted at least thirty-five shootable animals. While most were very impressive, I spotted one particular stag that had real possibilities. The heart pounding, throat-choking enthusiasm made it hard for Paul and me to keep our focus upon entertaining our wives and friends during the sumptuous dinner at the lodge. We silently stuffed the great grub into our mouths, periodically making eye contact long enough to catch one another's Cheshire Cat grin. We knew what excitement the next day would bring.

The Stalk

The chill of the early morning welcomed our senses to the clear, clean air of this pristine wilderness. The awe-inspiring hills and meadows surrounding the lodge provided a beautiful backdrop for our hunting day.

The scrub-covered gorges and expansive high meadows presented terrain ideal for both hunter and quarry. Fallow deer, sika deer, wild boar, exotic sheep, wild turkey, and a host of upland game birds were very visible in this majestic setting. Based on our previous day's initial scouting of the 5,000-acre private hunting area, we expected that our goal of taking a fourteen-point (or better) stag could be realized.

Paul and a couple of our other guests hooked up with one of the guides; the rest, including my wife and me, were assigned a masterguide, Richard, originally from Scotland. We were developing a booth video for Tree Tops and had our cameraman, Craig Lee, tracking with us to record all the action.

The morning sun began to warm the cool fall air as long shadows painted the mountainsides. Richard suggested we hunt an area near the place where he had seen a few bigger stags. There we would find several wallow areas and some heavy brush that tends to attract bigger animals.

We moved along in a stealthy fashion as we carefully peered around every bush and tree to catch a glimpse of a great monarch. My heart pounded with expectant joy as I wondered how many other top-ten stags might be on this property. My palms and brow were sweating as my camouflage makeup began to run down my face. I clung to my bow, knowing that at any moment I might need to nock an arrow. I moved on several animals, all within thirty yards. I passed on each one, waiting to find the bigger stag. The sheer size of these critters caused me to wonder if I shouldn't have cranked my bow up to the seventy-pound limit. My elbow surgery a few years earlier dictated that I keep my pull weight at sixty-two pounds.

We worked our way along the western face of a slope about midway up the mountain. Moving ever so quietly, stopping only to glass the territory before us, we listened carefully, evaluating every sound and movement. We happened upon our friends James and Betty Robison, who had spotted several nice deer but felt the climb would present too great a challenge for the ailing knee injury James was dealing with.

The occasional deafening roar of these big stags continued to make my pulse race. I remember thinking that the long climb would be no problem for my adrenaline-enriched body. Within minutes our vision fixed on a stag with massive antlers. Richard looked him over and said the stag fit our profile for a "trophy animal."

Our stalk to the deer was going to be difficult because of the open space separating us from his location. We used a few bushes on the upper slope that could help conceal our movements. We hunkered down and slowly crawled our way up the grade. After some maneuvering to get the wind in our favor, we moved closer to the herd.

My trophy animal came to the edge of the bluff as he looked over the terrain for any sign of danger. I had never seen an animal with such a crown of glory. He looked and acted like royalty. His posture and attitude typified a king surveying his empire for approval.

I sat in a couched position gazing at the majestic beast. Richard eased his way up to my position and whispered, "Hey, Jim, I think he is the one. Can you hit him from here?"

Looking at the stag uphill, he appeared farther away than he really was. The combination of the grade and his magnificent profile on the horizon caused me to estimate his range at fifty-five yards.

I nocked an arrow and carefully pulled the bow, hoping the slight movement wouldn't alert the animal. Ever so slowly, I inched my way to a full standing position as I centered my sixty-yard pin just above his back. The release was smooth as the arrow tracked its way toward the upper shoulder of the stag.

Just when I thought I had the perfect shot, the arrow slid over his back and crashed into the woods behind the great beast. His instincts took over as he leaped into the middle of the herd and sped off to a meadow area. I was very disappointed in myself for having misjudged the distance. It was clear that this critter was ten yards closer than I expected.

I replayed the shot over and over again, wondering how I could have blown such a great opportunity. The older stag was a grand specimen, 400 to 450 pounds with a large rack. His sixteen-point antlers, which would eventually total about 300 points SCI, qualified him as a "gold medal contender." While it was not a top-ten record book animal, it was without a doubt the largest deer I had ever stalked.

We continued following the herd until dark. The great deer never really allowed us another close-in opportunity.

Though we were very disappointed, the replay of the video showed that we had done many things right.

With Disappointment Comes New Hope

The next day brought new hope. Most of my group seemed to have no problem harvesting their twelve- to four-teen-point representative stag trophies with a rifle. With a few hours of light remaining, our guide asked if I was ready to commence the bow hunt for our trophy stag. I had resighted my bow and felt more confident about my chances. After a few hours of a cat-and-mouse stalk, we knew that the herd was aware of our interest in their activities.

My stag seemed to continually place himself in such a way that other deer became his shields and protectors. There were two fallow hinds (females) and one large red stag hind that continued to search the landscape for unwanted guests. From some distance, Richard and I once again planned a stalk. We moved along a deep trench and eased our way toward the herd. The lookouts spotted us and quickly moved the group upwind of our position.

To pressure them any more would be to frighten the group farther away, so we stayed in the ditch. We knew they would eventually make their way back to the grassy meadow—we just waited. The lush clover and irrigated grass provided them with a prime feeding area. As predicted, one by one the deer returned to the meadow. They passed by our concealed position unaware that we were tracking their every move. Our covered area provided a unique view of the activities of this magnificent herd. The perspective we had on the situation allowed us to make judgments and decisions that would affect the ultimate outcome.

We waited several minutes for the "big guy" to appear. Richard whispered, "Hey mate, we either missed seeing him or he and his female companions are still in the woods. I think we need to move in and check it out."

I realized that we had about one hour left for my hunt before dark. Richard and I moved into a small clearing among a number of larger trees. Approximately 125 yards from our position stood the majestic beast. Clearing the brush and chewing on its food, the old stag peered our way but could not pick up our scent since the wind was in our favor. Our lack of motion and full camouflage gear confused him long enough to give me the opportunity to thoroughly check him out through my binoculars.

Richard leaned over to pass along his observation: "I know you could ultimately take this guy with your bow, but we need another day to accomplish that task."

Our commitments to visiting other attractions dictated an early departure the next morning. I knew this was my last chance at the big guy.

"The whirling wind, level terrain and lookouts are not in our favor for this final stalk," Richard said. "John wants you to leave with a stag, so please use my 270 mm to take him down."

I must have seemed transfixed by the animal as I carefully studied every aspect of this great monarch, and as I paused to evaluate the options. With great reluctance I gave Richard my bow and positioned myself for the rifle shot.

The gun was poised at the ready as I rethought the possibility of continuing my bow stalk. As a hunter, I know there are times when a bow is not the most effective way to take an animal, but I had hoped that my trophy stag wasn't going to be one of those times.

While looking through the gun scope, I drifted into a state of reflection. I thought about how blessed I was to have this unique opportunity. I thought about the magnificence of this royal deer and how they have adapted so well to the productive New Zealand environment.

Richard interrupted my daydreaming with a reality check. The hinds had picked up our scent with the change of wind direction. They had stopped feeding and were sniffing the air. The hair on their backs was standing up, and their legs had become tense. I knew it was now or never. As the big stag began to turn downhill, my rifle barked out. The shot hit home. The stag reeled about five yards, and then rolled over on his side. Richard broke his concentration and smiled. "Congratulations, mate, you have joined an elite group of hunters."

As we moved toward the animal, I began to realize how big he was. I asked Richard to give me a few minutes alone with the stag before we started field-dressing him. After thanking God for delivering this trophy, I began to reflect on Richard's congratulatory remarks and the unique privilege of hunting this noble monarch. The isolation of this species in New Zealand was worth pondering before any further celebrating occurred. I wanted to discuss with Richard the past that was directly linked to the thrill of taking this great stag.

Consider the Past

In almost a meditative trance, I considered every word Richard had used to describe the elite fraternity of hunters who have taken this patriarch of all deer. I learned that prior to the animal's liberation in New Zealand, only a handful of European nobility had ever had the opportunity to hunt this elusive trophy on selected estates. Clearly, there is no antlered monarch that can match the prestige and intrigue of the red stag. It is steeped in folklore and tradition that rival tales of any revered African game or even the highly esteemed American elk.

The story of big-game hunting in New Zealand is unique in the archives of game management. The lush, subtropical environment greeted the original European colonists to New Zealand, but the only animals available to the settlers were some bats and a few small colonies of seals along the coastline. When early British pioneers surveyed the natural resources of this two-island country, they wanted to turn it into a sportsman's paradise. To that end, they imported a large variety of the world's best game and fish. One result was exceptional trophies.

Memories of Monarchs

Over the course of the last two years, I have reflected on the memories of that great trip. Dozens of friends have visited Tree Tops and had similar experiences. Each hunter made his way into the record book with a magnificent stag.

My research on the red stags has enabled me to meet many folks who share my zeal for this incredible animal. Of particular interest to everyone was the story behind the world-record stag shot in early 1991. I spoke with the operator and the guide, as well as the hunter, former Prince Japto Socrjosomarno of Indonesia, who took the gigantic 455-point deer. Memories of the hunt linger with all associated with that historical event.

"I have never experienced anything like this in my life," Japto says. "The stag was absolutely unbelievable." The magnificence of that great animal is the envy of any hunter who has heard the story or seen the pictures.

To anyone who knows the majesty and splendor of the Creator—God Almighty—this deer or any other marvelous hunting experience is but a speck of sand in a heavenly oasis.

God Almighty

When I think of things that are really awesome and mighty, nothing compares to the magnificence of God. We can talk all day long about 450-point red stags, or 350-point bull elk, but there is no equal to the significance of the Almighty. The words majestic, regal, royal and unique are pale-colored adjectives when it comes to describing the multifaceted character of God.

The various names of God are designations for His attributes. It is significant that names given to God are most often related to His people's needs. God is compassionate in the presence of our misery. He is long-suffering in the presence of our sinfulness. Our Lord provides grace in the presence of guilt. When we are repentant, the Almighty provides mercy. As He feels our needs, God can enter our lives with the appropriate comforting attribute.

The ancient Hebrews so respected God that they had great difficulty picking one word to describe the various attributes associated with His being. The names, titles, and metaphors for God in the Old Testament reflect Israel's cultural setting in the ancient Near East.

During their day there was great significance attached to personal names, for they revealed character and identity that added significance to God's existence.

Many times in the Old Testament, the people of God were called to remember all the good things God did for them. They often reflected upon the Lord Himself—His greatness, His grace, His goodness. It is helpful to recall some of the names for God in the Bible—Jehovah (or *Yahweh*), *Abba, El, El Shaddai* and *Elohim*—which point to the nature of God as being everlasting, infinite in power, absolute in faithfulness and perfect in holiness.

Out of reverence to his quarry, an experienced hunter honors a trophy animal with expressions of endearment. We often hear folks describe the regal trophies with names like "Royal Bull Elk," "Heavily Broomed Rams," "Old Scarface," "Legendary Buck," and "Trophy Stag."

In the Old Testament the priests and prophets revered God and acknowledged Him with different names. There were three common and distinct names for God that were most cherished by those who had entered into a personal relationship with Him. The word "God" most often translates into Hebrew as *El* (or the plural form, *Elohim*), the general Semitic term for deity, which is probably derived from a root denoting power or strength.[1]

I regarded that royal stag as powerful and noble because of his presence. In a similar fashion, during Old Testament times folks who had experienced God's presence and wanted to focus upon His supremacy would acknowledge Him with the word *El*.

Elohim means "the one supreme deity." It conveys the notion that everything belongs to the God most high. *Elohim* was the most common name for God.[2]

Another of the most recognized names for God in the Old Testament is *Yahweh*, from the verb "to be," meaning simply but profoundly, "He is." His full name is found only in Exodus 3:14 and means "I am who I am" or "I will be who I will be." The Hebrew word *Yahweh* is usually translated "the Lord" and sometimes "Jehovah." The original Hebrew text was not vocalized in ancient time because it was considered too sacred to pronounce. The word "Jehovah" was substituted for *Yahweh* and later translated into Greek in the early Christian church.

Yahweh was the God of the patriarchs. We read that *Yahweh* was the God of Abraham, then of Isaac and Jacob (Exodus 3:15). *Yahweh*, later Jehovah, presents God as a divine Person seeking a relationship with His creation.

It is interesting to consider the words used in His "face to face" meeting with Moses. He used all three words listed above to express His character: "I, the Lord [*Yahweh*] your God [*Elohim*], am a jealous God [*El*], punishing the children for the sin of the fathers to the third and fourth generation of those who hate me" (Deuteronomy 5:9).

Much as a great hunter learns to appreciate and respect his quarry, so, too, a child of God needs to value the complex and comforting character of God. Excerpts from Psalm 83 help us appreciate God's magnificence: "Keep not thou silence, O God: hold not thy peace, and be not still, O God. For lo, thine enemies make a tumult" (Psalm 83:12 KJV). The Psalmist proceeds to describe the enemies of Israel and the number of threats against the children of God. As the psalm winds down we see the reverence shown to God: "So persecute them with thy tempest, and make them afraid with thy storm. Fill their faces with shame, that they may seek thy name, O Lord. Let them be confounded and troubled for ever; yea, let them be put to shame and perish: That men may know that thou, whose name alone is JEHOVAH, art the most high over all the earth" (Psalm 83:15-18 KJV).

You ask, "How will knowing all these theological terms help me grow closer to God?"

The answer, my friend, deals with our ability to gain a greater understanding of a personal God who wishes to have deep fellowship with His creation. His diverse character is a source of rationality in a very confused and sinful world. In the full abundance of His nature, God transcends the universe—yet He manifests Himself in each attribute we come to know.

Pause a moment to "sight in" on a few of His qualities and feel the comfort and peace it brings to know that our God is more real than any trophy stag. Study them as carefully as you would any quarry, knowing that *this* trophy is measured in terms of eternal value. A relationship with God can be permanently mounted on the wall of your heart.

The great Jehovah wants a relationship with you. Appreciate some of the qualities associated with His imminence. He is near to you this day.

Jehovah-jireh—This name is translated as "The LORD Will Provide," commemorating the provision of the ram in place of Isaac for Abraham's sacrifice (Genesis 22:14).

Jehovah-nissi—This name means "The LORD Is My Banner," in honor of God's defeat of the Amalekites (Exodus17:15).

Jehovah-shalom—This phrase means "The LORD Is Peace," the name Gideon gave the altar that he built in Ophrah (Judges 6:24).

Jehovah-shammah—This phrase expresses the truth that "The LORD Is There," referring to the city the prophet Ezekiel saw in his vision (Ezekiel 48:35).

Jehovah-tsebaoth—This name, translated "The LORD of Hosts," was used in the days of David and the prophets, witnessing to the Almighty God of sovereign power who is served by armies of angels (1 Samuel 17:45 NASB).

Next time you think about God, remember some of His many attributes. Bathe yourself in an appreciation for His divine nature. If you like to keep scores on your trophies, try keeping track of all the ways God wants to love and serve you. There is no better way to acknowledge God than to know and praise Him for His many attributes. Good hunting!

Personal Application

- What do you think the psalmist had in mind when he penned Psalm 83. Who or what was he hunting for?

- Because God is the kind of God He is, the Old Testament character Job wondered how a person could ever hope to approach Him, much less become right and acceptable before Him. Can a mere human being have a right relationship with a God who is perfectly holy, infinite, and mighty? Bildad echoed Job's question, saying, "How then can a man be righteous before God?" (Job 25:4; Matthew 19:16; Acts 16:30).

- The greatest Hunter of all time is God. He is hunting for man's heart and soul.

  Read Matthew 16:24-28

Chapter 3

Bears and Believers

The Goodness of God

Early spring is a magical time in northern Idaho. This is the time when the sweet spring vegetation fills the air with a perfume aroma. The beautiful June-berry scrubs are adorned with white flowers that provide a beautiful contrast to the velvet green carpet of annual grasses that are evident in all the open areas.

I had recently moved to the Northwest and found that springtime in Northern Idaho is known for its superb black bear hunting. From my office window I could see the wildlife was becoming very active after a long, cold winter. I knew that the availability of so much food tempted the hibernating animals to indulge. Animals like the elusive black bear would be on the prowl for a good meal.

While this was appealing to me, my winter and spring schedules had been quite hectic and afforded me little opportunity to properly scout the best areas.

A local pastor contacted me about a speaking engagement for his church and asked if a "guided bear-hunting trip" would be enough incentive to compensate for my normal speaking fees. I graciously accepted and set a time to work in a hunt between commitments.

On my drive to the Sandpoint, Idaho, area, I remember sharing a request of God that went something like, "Dear God, because You are in control of all things I know You can deliver a bear to me if You desire. I have worked very hard in ministry this past year and would really appreciate a chance to take a good bear. I know this is somewhat of a selfish and insignificant request, but it would please my heart so to be allowed the privilege of harvesting one of these wonderful critters. Your Word tells us that You like to give a righteous man the desires of his heart. And so, my Lord, I humbly ask You to assist us with this hunt."

Upon arriving in Sandpoint, I met Clint Gray, a very talented young guide, who had just purchased Buck Shot Outfitting. His background and education in fish and wildlife management plus his forestry work had prepared him well for the opportunity to help guide folks into some rugged terrain. While most outfitters in this area use bait as a way to attract their bears, Clint believes in spotting and stalking as a challenging way to take a bear.

Upon my arrival I was greeted with the news that early scouting reports didn't look very good. It seemed that because of an unusually heavy snowfall, the early grasses were just beginning to appear.

Clint lamented, "The bears went into hibernation early due to an unseasonable snowfall and lack of food. They also came out early but very thin. The grass areas are very spotty and provide limited food supply for the hungry bears."

The first night we surveyed with our binoculars (glassed) several wooded areas and finally found a bear working the upper edge of a grassy hillside about two miles from our location. We only had two hours of light left. This gave us barely enough time to scamper up the steep, brushy bank. We planned our stalk to climb a section of mountain that would come out about a quarter-mile from where the bear was positioned.

As we worked our way through the heavy downfall, we knew our presence was being announced with the periodic snapping of dry limbs and debris. I remember that it was like walking on a conveyor belt covered with potato chips. As we crept around the dense vegetation separating us from the feeding bear, our confident expectation that the bear would still be there was quickly eliminated. Sure enough, the bear was no longer holding in the same location. Clint reckoned that "most likely he heard us stalking through the heavy timber and departed with the first snap of a twig."

The disappointing hike back to the truck gave us plenty of time to remember that spotting and stalking bear was a challenging exercise at best. The darkness of the evening covered our look of defeat.

The next morning we began scouting a variety of areas with no success. We saw plenty of signs but no bear. The late afternoon approached with a cold front and a small storm that further hampered our efforts in locating bear. As Clint began asking me questions about when I would again have time to come up and do some hunting, I realized that without assistance from the Creator this trip would be recorded in Clint's guide book as "an opportunity to get plenty of exercise."

After strolling through a couple of areas and seeing no sign, Clint decided to check out one more area before we headed home. The previous year, while doing a timber job, he had seen a nice chocolate bear in that area. We pulled our truck onto a dirt road and parked at a gate. The short walk to the meadow was filled with silence as both of us felt exhaustion and disappointment from hunting since 5:00 A.M.

After about ten minutes, I could see the open area at the end of the path. I decided to quietly chamber a round and put on my safety. The sun was beginning to set, and the remaining light was only going to last another few minutes. We carefully moved along the perimeter looking for any dark, fuzzy objects. As we initially peered around the field, we did not see anything that looked too promising.

We moved to a slightly higher elevation and began to search the area using my Nikon low-light binoculars and scope. As I studied the far end of the meadow, I thought I saw the shape of a bear. In a whisper I asked Clint, "Is that a bear or a stump?" Clint gazed through my binoculars and smiled as he said, "Sure enough, Jim! I think that is that big, chocolate-colored male bear (boar) I saw last year!" Knowing that we only had minutes left of legal shooting time, I decided not to try to close the distance by crawling across the meadow to get a close-in pistol shot with my .44 magnum as I had initially planned.

Instead we elected to move up a little higher where I could sneak behind a woodpile that could be used to steady a 100-yard rifle shot. Just as we were relocating, the bear looked up from his feeding. Our movement announced the fact that he was no longer the only one in this meadow. The big boar scampered into the woods where he could further analyze this situation.

I could faintly see the bear outlined against the darkened forest. His clumsy movements in the dense vegetation gave us the advantage by identifying his position. He peered through the underbrush and periodically stood up to try and catch our scent. The slight breeze in our faces provided some assurance that his efforts to identify us through smell would be hampered.

As minutes passed, my disappointment grew. I became frustrated at the thought that we had blown a chance to finally bag a trophy bear. As I heard the crunching sound of his lumbering steps moving farther into the woods, I could only think about what might have been.

I lowered my rifle to take a deep breath and reflect upon our impatient movements that might have frightened this critter. I looked at Clint and shook my head. He could read the disappointment on my face.

Even though it appeared hopeless, we both stood rigid, minutes passed as we peered into the blackness. Suddenly we again heard the familiar sounds of a large animal blundering its way back to the meadow. The fuzzy, dark image again appeared along the perimeter of the woods, just to the left of where we had first seen it. I gazed at the animal with disbelief. I now had some understanding of how Abraham must have felt when God delivered the ram to be sacrificed for his son Isaac. I felt very blessed that God's providence would allow us a second chance to take this grand bear.

Clint and I stared at the bear without saying a word. As soon as the bear moved sideways and commenced feeding, I slipped in front of Clint for the shot. From a standing off-hand position, I steadied my aim and gently squeezed the trigger when the bear stepped into my crosshairs. My Browning 7 mm barked as the Boss Muzzle Break System dissipated the flash into the cold night air.

The flash temporarily took away my evening vision. The piercing noise seemed to awaken the sleepy forest as critters starting yelping and chirping. Clint yelled out with joy, "You hit him, Jim, you hit him!"

As my eyes adapted again to the dark shadows, I peered through my scope to see the bear gasping for its last breath. I fired another round to quickly end the drama. We dashed to the fallen animal with a sense of thankfulness and wonder. To know that the Creator was gracious enough to redirect this bear our way was a humbling exercise.

As I knelt down to thank God for His goodness, I was reminded how gracious our God is to provide so many things. The Psalmist reminds us that nothing escapes His attention "He provides food for the cattle and for the young ravens when they call" (Psalm 147:9).

Even the simple request of a tired hunter was seen and responded to with a loving heart.

God takes great delight in providing gifts to His children. He loves surprising us with bounty beyond our imaginations. "And we know that in all things God works for the good of those who love him, who have been called according to his purpose" (Romans 8:28).

This unique adventure caused me to think about the words found in Scripture that defined Abraham's experience: "Abraham looked up and there in a thicket he saw a ram caught by its horns. He went over and took the ram and sacrificed it as a burnt offering instead of his son. So Abraham called that place The Lord Will Provide. And to this day it is said, 'On the mountain of the Lord it will be provided' " (Genesis 22:13,14).

The goodness of God is neverending. It is when we examine His acts of goodness that we see more of His character.

Understanding the Goodness of God

Someone once said, "Goodness consists not so much in the outward things we do but in the inward things we are." As we further study the character of God, we see that the inward things that constitute His divine character include a heart of being good to His creation.

The awesomeness of God often causes us to fear Him. His goodness encourages us not to fear but to appreciate His kindness and cordiality. It is a paradox of our faith to fear God but not to be afraid. It is through understanding His loving nature and His goodness that we are able to appreciate His infinite care.

The goodness of God is defined through His kindness, benevolence and acts of good will toward mankind. His blessings, mercy, sympathy and tenderheartedness can be seen throughout Scripture and in our daily living. The reality that God is good is taught or implied on every page of the Bible. Some would say it is the foundation for understanding the basic nature of God. If God is not good, then there can be no distinction between kindness and cruelty, or between heaven and hell.

When Jesus was asked about the goodness of God, He replied, "Why do you ask me about what is good?...There is only One who is good. If you want to enter life, obey the commandments" (Matthew 19:17).

It is the goodness of God that drives the appreciation for the many daily blessings we receive. Blessings like a bear coming back out of the woods so that a tired hunter might have some meat for his freezer and the joy of taking a trophy bear. We need to appreciate those unexpected pleasures of life that cause us to humble ourselves before man and God.

Since God is unchanging and perfect in His character, we can appreciate that the intensity of His goodness and lovingkindness is the same yesterday, today, and tomorrow. He has never been kinder than He is now. He will not become more kind in His character in the future. He is no respecter of persons but makes His sun to shine on the just and unjust alike.

Somehow in the unique character of the Almighty there exists the potential to be just and fair while continuing to be good. It is that mystical blend of God's being that enables Him to stand in judgment of man while continuing to show mercy.

The goodness of God can be seen in many ways. His character serves as a model for us to follow in knowing how we can manifest goodness to others. "You are good, and what you do is good; teach me your decrees" (Psalm 119:68).

God's Goodness Supplies Temporal Wants

"Yet he has not left himself without testimony: He has shown kindness by giving you rain from heaven and crops in their seasons; he provides you with plenty of food and fills your hearts with joy" (Acts 14:17).

God delights in providing goodness to His creation. By supplying us with our temporal wants, He demonstrates His compassion for creation. In His divine plan for mankind God provided "all things" and an ability to willfully choose our destiny. These things are a testimony of His goodness and creative powers. God is not a control freak. He has graciously made us with spirits and minds so that we can choose our fate.

God's Goodness Leads to Repentance

"Or do you show contempt for the riches of his kindness, tolerance and patience, not realizing that God's kindness leads you toward repentance?" (Romans 2:4).

The natural response to someone who has demonstrated kindness is to show appreciation. We can demonstrate appreciation in many ways. Once we accept God's goodness in our life, we have a responsibility to analyze our attitudes and actions in light of His unmerited favor. Most people have a desire to change their behavior as a testimony of their thankfulness for His goodness.

Our verbal acknowledgement of the act is always appropriate. When this is expressed to our divine Creator, we call it prayer. A repentant heart (changed life) can testify and thank God for the goodness and mercy given in a specific situation.

God's Goodness Is Expressed in His Forgiveness

"Although most of the many people who came from Ephraim, Manasseh, Issachar and Zebulun had not purified themselves, yet they ate the Passover, contrary to what was written. But Hezekiah prayed for them, saying, 'May the LORD, who is good, pardon everyone'" (2 Chronicles 30:18).

Like King Hezekiah, we want to cry out to our loving and faithful God to thank Him for His grace and His mercy. Out of God's goodness He answers prayer and forgives sin.

"You are forgiving and good, O Lord, abounding in love to all who call to you" (Psalm 86:5).

It is because of God's goodness that He allows us access to His eternal kingdom. By accepting the wonderful gift of salvation we can have the forgiveness of sin. I would think that Christ's sacrifice on the cross was the ultimate act of goodness from a loving God. He asks each one of us to accept and appreciate this act for its transforming power. Have you accepted this act of goodness from God?

As we endeavor to model God's character, let us do good. We can do more good by being good than in any other way. In the final analysis, the only way to be good is to obey God.

"Let us not become weary in doing good, for at the proper time we will reap a harvest if we do not give up" (Galatians 6:9).

John Bunyan once said, "Everyone will cry up the goodness of men; but who is there that is, as he should, affected with the goodness of God?"[1]

Are we daily demonstrating the goodness of God in our lives? What acts of goodness have you provided to others this day?

Personal Application

- How can God's character serve as a model for us to follow in knowing how we can manifest goodness to others? "You are good, and what you do is good; teach me your decrees" (Psalm 119:68).

- When Jesus was asked about the goodness of God, He replied, "Why do you ask me about what is good?... There is only One who is good. If you want to enter life, obey the commandments" (Matthew 19:17). What does that mean in terms of how you should live your life?

Chapter 4

Bull Elk

The God of Grace

Most people who know Dr. John MacArthur would testify that he is one of the hardest-working clergymen in the world. The greater part of his life has been devoted to studying God's Word and developing some of the most insightful resource materials I have ever seen.

His Bible teaching program "Grace to You" is aired more than 1,200 times a day in almost every English-speaking country. It is clear that many consider his international radio ministry one of the best teaching series in the world.

A little-known fact about Pastor John is his unbelievable success when it comes to outdoor activities. His record-book achievements make even the most ardent sportsmen shake their heads in disbelief.

Several years ago, two of John's friends encouraged him to join them on an elk-hunting trip in eastern Oregon. Pastor John admits, "I wasn't really interested in the hunt as much as the opportunity to get away and enjoy God's great outdoors with my friends Jerry Smith and Jim Rickard." His friends wanted John to have the experience of hunting for an elk even though their pastor's hunting experience was limited to shooting a couple of rabbits when he was younger.

John recalls, "They handed me a 7 mm rifle and a pair of binoculars. The instruction consisted of them saying to me, 'Look through the binoculars and if you see something that looks like a big deer; then we will line him up in the scope of the gun and pull the trigger.' "

The Unearned Gift

Though John is a person of great faith, he knew that this adventure was a real shot in the dark. To even see an elk within the limited time he had with these guys might be called a miracle.

The group started out early in the morning and began their drive along an old riverbed. According to John, "It was a cool winter morning as we started down the creek-bed riding in our four-wheel-drive vehicle. I was looking over the landscape with the binoculars, when, about an hour into the trip, I saw something about 300 yards away at the top of the ridge. I told the guys, 'I think I see a big elk!' With disbelief written all over their face, Jim grabbed the binoculars and looked up the steep hill.

"Jim shouted out, 'Sure enough, that is a dandy bull elk!' It is a great six-by-six animal. Jerry suggested that we try a shot from the hood of the truck. The bipod on the rifle would help stabilize the gun for the long shot."

John had never even fired this particular gun before, let alone a large-caliber weapon like a 7 mm. The reluctant pastor peered through the scope and saw the huge animal slowly walking parallel to their position. When he stopped, his head was behind a big tree.

"I think the elk thought he was out of harm's way because his head was concealed. He didn't realize that his entire side was exposed and presented me with a great heart shot on his left side."

John jokes about his novice approach to sighting in on the elk. "I never knew what 'buck fever' was until I tried to focus on the animal. I felt a shortness of breath, my heart felt like it was up in my throat, and my knees began to shake. I had to stop and take a deep breath in order to calm myself while again getting the elk in my scope. I remember the angle of the shot was pretty steep. After taking a few times to set myself, I squeezed the trigger."

The recoil of the rifle placed the scope right in John's forehead, opening a big cut above his eye. "I remember that blood was flowing everywhere. The guys seemed more concerned with me than if I even hit the animal. Once we determined that I was going to be okay, Jerry grabbed the binoculars and said, 'Well, I'll be! He is down! Can you believe that a guy who has never really tried for a trophy elk could shoot a critter like this in the first hour out?'"

As John began his hike up to the deceased animal, he thought about the grace of God.

"This hunt was so amazing because I didn't deserve any of the blessings God gave me on this trip. I thought about the graciousness of our loving God for giving me this marvelous animal."

Knowing a God of Grace

Pastor John MacArthur is considered one of the top Bible scholars of our time. As a renowned pastor-teacher, college president and Christian radio personality, he has not always rested in the grace of God for his strength. Early in his career, he tried to achieve spiritual greatness with his own power and intellect. Then John began to focus upon the lessons taught in Matthew 11, where Jesus says, "Come to Me, all who are weary and heavy-laden, and I will give you rest. Take My yoke upon you, and learn from Me, for I am gentle and humble in heart; and you shall find rest for your souls. For My yoke is easy, and My load is light" (Matthew 11:28-30 NASB). The message Pastor John heard from Scripture settled in his heart and mind. He realized that power and greatness come from God. It is God's grace that empowers and equips people to fully utilize their abilities.

Pastor John believes the more you fill yourself with divine truth, the less impact your personal efforts, intellect and skills have on your life's work. There is a well of divine truth that enables us to fully utilize our God-given gifts and talents. Most mature believers have discovered that the more we are filled with the Holy Spirit, the more our efforts can become effortless.

The old hymn encourages our hearts with the kind words, "Amazing grace—how sweet the sound that saved a wretch like me!" Grace is a delightful word and a wonderful attribute of our loving God. If we are careful to study the traits of God and feel His presence in our lives, we can experience His continual kindness and compassion.

As we sort through the spiritual knapsack of Godlike traits we have collected on this journey, it would appear to the casual observer that grace and mercy are part of the same trait. But a closer study of God's character reveals that there is a clear distinction between the two. Mercy is God's goodness confronting human misery and guilt. Grace is His goodness directed toward our debt and demerit. Grace is the good pleasure of God that inclines Him to grant forgiveness and blessings upon an undeserving individual.[1]

Grace is a topic I really enjoy studying. When I think of how thankful I am for all the "unmerited favor" God has given me, I appreciate all the more the importance of His grace to the forgiveness of my sin. God took a tough, foul-mouthed teenager, who was full of anger, and gave him a heart of compassion and love. Much like Saul of Tarsus, I saw my life transformed by God's hope and forgiveness.

It is not often that I read or quote from a book written specifically for women. My wife urged me to consider one such book in reviewing my thoughts on grace. I truly enjoyed Cynthia Heald's insights in *Becoming a Woman of Grace*. She helps us understand how, from the beginning, God desired to be a Father of grace.

"From its opening pages, Scripture shows us that God has always longed to be gracious. His creation of a marvelous world out of nothing is amazing evidence of His grace, and He placed His children in it to be recipients of His grace. In the garden, Adam and Eve were immersed in God's goodness. They did nothing to earn their place there, and they did nothing to receive His love. God simply chose to be kind, merciful, and compassionate to them. Charles Ryrie observes, 'God's love for man is the first motive for His acting in grace on behalf of man.' From creation onward we find that God has showered upon us His undeserved favor. Truly He is the God of all grace." [2]

Are We Full of Grace?

There seems to be a great deal of confusion about one of the most fundamental doctrines of the Christian faith—grace. I see many denominations that are quick to discuss the importance of fearing God. Much of their liturgy demands that a follower obey God's every command. Many believers are quick to remind others that God is watching their every move and that followers "better watch out—God will get you." No wonder that those who have yet to receive Jesus as their personal Savior are not interested in pursuing such a threatening faith.

And those legalistic, judgmental believers who often set the rules and interpret the ordinances are really no better than the first-century Pharisees and Sadducees. By their indignant attitudes and actions they are grace-killers. Most of the time these folks miss out on the joy of their faith because they are too worried about messing up.

Jesus came to set us free, to release us for service. He wants us to enjoy our faith and live the abundant life. The Protestant Reformation was about a group of people who realized that Christianity should be built upon grace, not upon guilt. In fact, grace is foundational for faith itself. Jesus said, "I am the way and the truth and the life. No one comes to the Father except through me" (John 14:6). The very act of the Father encouraging us to have faith is a gracious consideration.

If God were to quickly punish every hunter who has ever broken any law, we would find very few people in the woods. His gracious and patient approach to encouraging and loving His creation is truly amazing. God's grace is truly incomprehensible and undeniable.

My friend Pastor Wayne Barber in his insightful book *The Rest of Grace,* writes about the principles associated with law and grace: "Law and grace work under two different principles, although the standard does not change: God still demands perfection and purity from us. Under law, it is up to me to attain it. Under grace, He has put His Spirit within me to enable me to attain it. The difference is that while I live under grace, I am enabled to do what God has commanded me to do."[3]

Think about the simple yet profound truths that bring us to faith. "Consequently, just as the result of one trespass was condemnation for all men, so also the result of one act of righteousness was justification that brings life for all men. For just as through the disobedience of the one man the many were made sinners, so also through the obedience of the one man the many will be made righteous" (Romans 5:18,19).

"For God so loved the world that he gave his one and only Son, that whoever believes in him shall not perish but have eternal life" (John 3:16).

My friend, these verses and many others are about a gracious God who allows us the privilege of entering into a holy relationship without being a perfect person.

Can coming to faith and being accepted into the kingdom of God for all eternity be that simple? It is, and that's why we call it *God's grace*. Does the Bible tell us that all we have to do is believe Jesus died for our sins, ask Him to forgive our transgressions, and receive Him as Lord of our lives? That's it! God provides heavenly *grace* for all who genuinely repent of their sins and confess Him as their Savior.

The Unearned Gift

"If ever there was an undeserving hunter, it was me," Pastor John says. "I paid no dues, bought no weapon, I didn't invest any money, I had no training, and I didn't earn this trophy elk in any way. Yet God blessed me with this opportunity. I got my reward by grace," he says. "On that day, I just managed to be blessed. For me grace is God giving us what we don't deserve, what we couldn't earn, and what we can't achieve on our own."

The same thing happened to John when he went on his first fishing trip with Bassmaster Ray Scott. After a few minutes of instruction, John made a cast and caught his first bass, which ended up being a ten-pounder. John will be the first to admit, "Once again, that was just God's grace being demonstrated in a very tangible way."

Charles Swindoll offers a good working definition of grace: "To show grace is to extend favor or kindness to one who doesn't deserve it and can never earn it. Receiving God's acceptance by grace always stands in sharp contrast to earning it on the basis of works. Every time the thought of grace appears, there is the idea of its being undeserved. In no way is the recipient getting what he or she deserves. Favor is being extended simply out of the goodness of the heart of the giver... It is absolutely and totally free. You will never be asked to pay it back. You couldn't even if you tried." [4]

Is this a one-time deal? Salvation is, but not grace. God's sustaining mercy, compassion, leniency, and forgiveness are ongoing for all who believe. He is with us to empower and strengthen through His giving of grace. James D. Mallory Jr. states, "Many Christians seem to understand the concept of being saved by grace, but they have missed the concept of being sustained by grace." [5]

I'm Just an Old, Depraved Hunter

If you're about ready to turn to a new chapter because you feel your actions and attitudes are not worthy of grace, I encourage you to read on. Because God is gracious, sinful man is forgiven, converted, purified, and saved. It is not because of anything we do but because of the infinite love, mercy, goodness, pity, compassion, and grace of God.

How big is the grace of God? Who can measure its breadth? Who can fathom its depth? As with all other divine attributes of God, His spreading of grace is infinite.

Have you persecuted, tortured, and even participated in killing others for their beliefs? Have you blasphemed the very name of our Lord? Sounds pretty bad, right? Could God really forgive someone who did all that? Yes, He could, and He did.

Read a quick summary of the life of Paul, formerly called Saul from Tarsus, the persecutor: "For I am the least of the apostles and do not even deserve to be called an apostle, because I persecuted the church of God. But by the grace of God I am what I am, and his grace to me was not without effect. No, I worked harder than all of them—yet not I, but the grace of God that was with me. Whether, then, it was I or they, this is what we preach, and this is what you believed" (1 Corinthians 15:9-11).

Placing This Attribute in My Knapsack

The late pastor and Bible scholar Donald Barnhouse said, "Love that goes upward is worship; love that goes outward is affection; love that stoops is grace."[6] Living a life of grace in a critical culture is not always easy. Our driven society is one that worries about perfectionism and mistakes but often forgets about grace. If a professional baseball player gets a hit once every three times up at bat, we place him in the Hall of Fame. If a basketball player shoots 50 percent, he most likely will make the Dream Team. If a quarterback has more touchdown passes than interceptions, ESPN will be interviewing him on a regular basis. If a hunter gets an animal every second time out, he is considered a masterhunter.

Yet in our own lives we sometimes project a critical spirit, a smothering kind of control towards others. We sometimes cultivate a sense of discouragement and fear that can affect trust and loyalty. Occasionally, we intimidate others through our position or power. Maybe someone has offended us, and we just can't forgive them for their trespass.

When we operate with these judgmental, legalistic attitudes, we most likely lack grace. Remember, grace is always kind and gentle, willing to quickly forgive and encourage.

People of Grace

Are we really people of grace? Sometimes we forget about grace in our passion to fulfill our goals, dreams and ambitions. In our efforts to succeed, conquer, or win, we can focus too much on the goal and forget the process. When the product becomes more important than the process, when relationships become secondary to acquiring position or power, most likely we have missed the opportunity to provide grace to someone.

I have known some folks who are very critical and legalistic in their assessment of others. They lack sensitivity in evaluating circumstances and problems. Many of these folks consider themselves great twenty-first-century managers because they are efficient, effective and critical. Unfortunately, they may be missing out on the opportunity to model a meaningful Christian life to others because they lack grace.

John Piper writes: "God is gracious to whom He will be gracious. He is not limited by anyone's wickedness. He is never trapped by His own wrath. His grace may break out anywhere He pleases." [7]

Final Shot for Grace

Pastor John emphasizes that it is "grace alone, my friend." We serve a very gracious God who enables us to do all things.

"Every good thing bestowed and every perfect gift is from above, coming down from the Father of lights, with whom there is no variation, or shifting shadow" (James 1:17 NASB).

Pastor John continues to faithfully serve, unaffected by achieving two of the top goals in the sporting world. He knows that his abilities and service are a blessing from a gracious God. His desire is to continue showing grace to others in the same way the apostle Paul demonstrated his thankfulness for the grace extended to him.

"Therefore, since we are receiving a kingdom which cannot be shaken, let us have grace, by which we may serve God acceptably with reverence and godly fear" (Hebrews 12:28 NKJ).

John Newton's eighteenth-century hymn "Amazing Grace" continues to be my favorite spiritual hymn. The power of his testimony, the message of man's release from sin grips my soul each time I sing it. Have you experienced God's grace? Are you providing that same grace to others?

Amazing grace! How sweet the sound!
That saved a wretch like me!

I once was lost, but now am found,
Was blind, but now I see.

'Twas grace that taught my heart to fear,
And grace my fears relieved;
How precious did that grace appear
The hour I first believed.[8]

Personal Application

- There are literally hundreds of verses in Scripture that describe grace. Slowly read just a few, and then ask yourself if you have truly accepted the grace God has given you. Are you a gracious person?

  "The law was given by Moses, but grace and truth came by Jesus Christ" (John 1:17 KJV).

  "By grace you are saved through faith" (Ephesians 2:8).

  "Where sin abounded, grace did much more abound" (Romans 5:20 KJV).

  "I am astonished that you are so quickly deserting the one who called you by the grace of Christ and are turning to a different gospel" (Galatians 1:6).

- The following list identifies some things we need to think about when extending grace to others:

  1. We can accomplish much through might and power, but it is more lasting to employ the Holy Spirit as our partner so that the product and results are of Him.

2. Rather than being critical, be expectant—provide a lot of encouragement and grace to others.

3. Be more tolerant and less judgmental—legalism is dead. Let's reach others with love and compassion.

4. Don't let a person's petty habits or attitudes get in the way of your showing them grace.

• Have you received the free gift of grace? If not, what stands in your way?

"Therefore, since we have been justified through faith, we have peace with God through our Lord Jesus Christ" (Romans 5:1).

• Legalistic people tend to twist the truth and project guilt instead of grace. How does Galatians 1:6-10 inspire you?

Chapter 5

This Little Piggy

God Is Merciful

The Napa/Sonoma Valley in northern California is known for its outstanding wines, beautiful scenery, and abundant wild boars. The oak woodland community, with its rolling, grass-covered hills, and abundant chaparral, is ideal habitat for this wilderness beast.

Originally released in this area during the early 1900s, the pigs adapted well to the favorable environment and modest hunting pressure. While their meat is very tasty, most California hunters would rather chase the various antlered critters than pursue the lowly pig. Consequently, hunting for these relatively unpressured animals can be a rewarding experience.

My good friend and hunting companion Jeff Klippenes is an exceptional hunter and brings a pioneering spirit into all his outdoor adventures. Jeff and a few of his friends have leased about 5,000 acres of farmland in this pristine area for their hunting activities. Over the past several years he has taken some real nice pigs but none as memorable as the 300-pounder he took on November 18, 1999.

Jeff recalls the auspicious day: "I went up to the ranch to sow clover for food plots. It was just one of those cool fall mornings when I started my chores."

As a native of northern Minnesota, Jeff loves to escape to the wilderness where he can commune with God. As a family therapist and pastor, he finds the time in the woods therapeutic for recuperating from the hectic pace of being a faithful servant.

It was about 10:45 in the morning when Jeff looked up from his tasks and saw a group of pigs feeding under a large oak tree. "I decided to grab my Matthews bow and see if I could stalk the group without them catching my scent."

After watching the mob for about fifteen minutes, Jeff closed the distance, checked his range finder and decided to launch an arrow about twenty yards from the pigs. "I saw it penetrate the big pig right behind the shoulder. I remember whacking him hard and then watching him just stroll off like nothing happened. This was the same setup I shot clean through a 715-pound elk at sixty-two yards. I couldn't believe my eyes that the arrow didn't kill him instantly."

The group of pigs seemed to continue lingering until the lead sow caught wind of Jeff. He was spotted, and the old sow became indignant that Jeff was invading their territory. "I knew I was in trouble when she gave me that look. They have that stare just before they charge. Within a split second I was up and running. I think that I could have probably outrun Carl Lewis at that point."

The sow chased Jeff right onto his Honda quad (a four-wheeled dirt bike). As Jeff sped off, the mud from his tires hit the old sow in the face. He moved downhill where he could observe the pigs in safety. He saw the brushy area his boar had moved into and knew that he would pick up a blood trail in that area.

Jeff continued to watch as the lead sow and remaining pigs moved to another area several hundred yards upwind from their original position. Jeff jumped back on the quad and made his way back to where he had fired the arrow at the big pig.

He quickly picked up the blood trail that led directly into a very brushy area. Wounded pigs will normally access heavy growth areas to escape their predators while putting the terrain in their favor.

Jeff began to belly crawl through the oak brush, dragging his bow behind him. "After twenty minutes I could tell I was about ten, fifteen yards from him, but I still couldn't see him. I heard him panting and an occasional squeal. I could tell he was hurt and angry.

"I stopped to think it over when I heard a small voice within, 'Jeff, this brush is so thick you can't even draw your bow back. Think about what you are doing. Get out of here now! Go get your rifle.'"

Jeff reversed his crawl and squeezed out of his brush tunnel. He walked back to his quad and drove down to camp continuing to think about the little voice that spoke to his soul. Grounded in the Word and open to the Spirit's leading, Jeff regularly welcomes the tender mercies of the Lord upon his life. Those little promptings of His Spirit help guide Jeff's life and allow him unique insights on his patients' lives.

After retrieving his gun, he returned to his crawl, feeling like a mole creeping through a burrow. Jeff spent more than forty-five minutes slowly crawling through the brush, carefully checking every opening for the sight of the big pig.

Jeff could sense that he was close to the critter. He carefully searched every opening, crevice and movement, hoping to pick up some clue as to the location of the pig. As his nostrils filled with the scent of the wet earth and his heart leaped to his throat, Jeff once again heard the small voice: "Stand up and stretch." The crawl and the stress of the event were settling into his back. Without warning he had developed a cramp in his low back that could be alleviated only by a good stretch. He peered to his right and saw a small opening where he could stand upright.

As soon as he was in the upright position, he heard a "whoff" and the sound of brush popping. He quickly yanked his gun from his backside and pointed the muzzle at the parting brush. Sliding the safety off with his thumb and wrapping his finger through the trigger guard, he fired a shot at the charging pig.

"In one motion I swung and fired, all the time trying to push back into the brush. I shot the pig at twelve to fourteen inches. The bullet caught the pig between the eyes, and he dropped at my feet. What a rush!"

The smoke cleared, and the sounds of nature returned to find Jeff standing in awe, amazed at what he had just experienced. It was clear that the mercies of the Lord were present in his situation. The still, small voice he heard transcended the moment. Had he not followed the directions of the Lord, he might have a permanent impression of a pig's snout on his forehead. After thanking God for his bounty, he boned the pig and slithered out of the brush with several pieces of pork ready for wrapping.

He figures that with a bow and arrow there isn't the concussion of a bullet to quickly knock a big pig over. He also learned that with big boar it takes a patient and quiet approach to stalk the pig or the opportunity will be missed.

Lessons Learned from a Pig in a Bush

Jeff experienced the mercy of God upon his life as he pursued that pig. Our merciful Father wished to spare the righteous life of this committed man. Jeff felt the presence of God in his decision-making and to this day continues to reflect upon the "still, quiet voice" that warned him of the impending danger.

Over the years, both Jeff and I have learned to listen to that inner voice that speaks to our subconscious. Age, experience, and waiting on God are teaching us to have eyes that see, ears that really hear, and a discerning wisdom so we can pick up on the subtle things God is showing us.

Like most people, we are so busy pushing to resolve problems or conflicts or to obtain success that we fail to take the time to be still and listen to God (Psalm 46:10). In the quiet moments of his entry into the brush tunnel, Jeff sought out God's voice to direct his steps. The wise counsel from the book of Proverbs tells us, "A simple man believes anything, but a prudent man gives thought to his steps" (Proverbs 14:15). Also, "If the LORD delights in a man's way, he makes his steps firm" (Psalm 37:23).

Jeff realized that by experiencing God's mercy he could also sense God's strong protective power and watchful eye. He really felt our Lord's inexhaustible compassion and infinite goodness as he reflected on what might have been. Because of his experience, he knew more about the character of God.

Many outdoorsmen consider incidents of adversity, challenges, or threats mere coincidences. Actually, it is by the grace and mercy of God that they were allowed to overcome or escape the perils.

When we ignore or take for granted our inner voice—the convictions or nudgings of God—we become reliant on our questionable judgment and vacillating feelings. The voice of God is anchored in His Word and in the guidance of the Holy Spirit. Christ left His Comforter (the Holy Spirit) to enable and assist us with daily decisions. If we have truly received Christ as our Savior and Lord, we can count on His Spirit to be our GPS for life.

A. W. Tozer reminds us, "God is merciful as well as just. He has always dealt in mercy with mankind and will always deal in justice when His mercy is despised." Regarding mercy, Tozer goes on to say, "As judgment is God's justice confronting moral iniquity, so mercy is the goodness of God confronting human suffering and guilt."[1]

God's Mercy for His Creation

Many folks seem to have a notion that justice and judgment characterize the God of the Old Testament, while mercy and grace belong to the Lord of the New Testament. The truth is that the Old Testament speaks four times more about mercy than the New Testament does.

While there are many great New Testament lessons taught on this subject, I consider the message given in the Old Testament book of Jonah to have some interesting similarities to Jeff's adventure. As we pack another trait of God in our spiritual knapsack, let us turn our attention to how Jonah's understanding of God's mercy changed after he worked through his trial.

God had given Jonah a mission to go to Nineveh. Nineveh was a great city both in size and in influence. It was probably among the largest cities in the world and greatly affected commerce in the Middle East. It had a population of more than 600,000 people who were predominantly idolaters. They worshipped the goddess Nanshe, a half-woman, half-fish idol.

It is estimated that more than 120,000 people lived there and could not yet discern good from evil (they could not tell their right hand from their left—see Jonah 4:11).

God had great mercy on this city and asked His prophet Jonah to go and start a revival of His Spirit in this evil place. But Jonah was frightened and decided to disobey God by getting on a ship headed in the opposite direction. So God intervened and directed a large fish to swallow Jonah after he was thrown overboard for his disobedience to God.

After Jonah repented, God mercifully placed him on the dry shoreline near Nineveh. Jonah began to preach and teach, and people began to believe in God. They fasted and put on sackcloth as a sign of humbling themselves before God.

God responded in mercy to man's repentance by canceling the threatened punishment He was going to give this evil land. Similarly, in Sodom, God was ready to spare the land from His wrath for just ten righteous people.

In Jonah 4, we pick up on Jonah's reaction and God's continued mercy. Jonah was displeased and even angry with God because of the grace and mercy He had shown to the Ninevites, the enemies of Israel. Jonah couldn't understand why God would show pity and compassion to such sinners. However, the repenting Nineveh had proved herself more worthy of God's favor than the children of the covenant who had fallen away from God's commands.

Jonah, depressed and confused, decides to go to the nearby hillside and sulk. He sits under a small shelter and waits for God's instructions. Jonah acknowledged God: "O LORD, is this not what I said when I was still at home? That is why I was so quick to flee to Tarshish. I knew that you are a gracious and compassionate God, slow to anger and abounding in love, a God who relents from sending calamity" (Jonah 4:2).

Jonah already knew this about God's character because of his own experience and the written record from his predecessors as described in Exodus 34 and Joel 2:13.

Because the shelter was small and the sun was beating down upon the prophet, God ordered up a small miracle as an illustration to Jonah of His mercy and faithfulness.

> *Then the LORD God provided a vine [a large leaf plant called a gourd] and made it grow up over Jonah to give shade for his head to ease his discomfort, and Jonah was very happy about the vine. But at dawn the next day God provided a worm, which chewed the vine so that it withered. When the sun rose, God provided a scorching east wind, and the sun blazed on*

Jonah's head so that he grew faint. He wanted to die, and said, "It would be better for me to die than to live." But God said to Jonah, "Do you have a right to be angry about the vine?"

"I do," he said. "I am angry enough to die."

"But the LORD said, "You have been concerned about this vine, though you did not tend it or make it grow. It sprang up overnight and died overnight. But Nineveh has more than a hundred and twenty thousand people who cannot tell their right hand from their left, and many cattle as well. Should I not be concerned [have pity or have mercy] about that great city?" (Jonah 4:6-11).

Zeroing in on Jonah, God asked him candidly if he had a right to be angry about the vine. God reminded Jonah that he had been "concerned" about the vine (or had looked upon the vine with compassion/pity)—something for which Jonah had not labored nor had he nurtured it to cause it to grow.

If Jonah had become so attached to a gourd (upon which he had expended no thought, no labor, no toil, no sacrifice, no care, no planting, no watering, no tending, no pruning), then why shouldn't God be concerned about the 600,000 Ninevites who were spiritually lost?

Certainly God's Word pierces our hearts even today as it confronts us with our prejudices, selfish attitudes, and unforgiving spirits. Many of us become so concerned with our own vines that we forget the "concerns" of God—the people for whom Christ died.

The God of Mercy

Many people in homes and communities throughout our country are a lot like Nineveh. They worship idols such as materialism, sex, power, and fame, only to feel empty at the end of the day. God's faithfulness and mercy await a repenting individual—or nation. If we are to be spared and to receive God's mercy, we must do what Scripture tells us. "If my people, who are called by my name, will humble themselves and pray and seek my face and turn from their wicked ways, then will I hear from heaven and will forgive their sin and will heal their land" (2 Chronicles 7:14).

During the life of the apostle Paul, Rome was an idol-worshipping community that found it difficult to repent. In his letter to the Christian church in Rome, Paul exhorts his brothers and sisters that, "Just as you who were at one time disobedient to God have now received mercy as a result of their disobedience, so they too have now become disobedient in order that they too may now receive mercy as a result of God's mercy to you. For God has bound all men over to disobedience so that he may have mercy on them all" (Romans 11:30-32).

God is saying through Paul that although He is not the author of sin, God has allowed man to pursue his sinful inclinations so that He can receive glory by demonstrating His grace and mercy to disobedient sinners.

In order for our hearts and our land to be healed by the grace and mercy of God, we must seek to be righteous. Jeff is a righteous person who "hears from heaven and has asked for forgiveness," and God has shown him mercy. My dear friend, God wants to heal your brokenness and speak to your heart. Like Jeff and many other friends who know God, you can listen to that small voice within that will guide and direct your paths. Like Jonah, there are times we need to sit under a tree or find that quiet place to listen to God.

Man is quick to forget God's miracles and mercies. The saving of hundreds of thousands of people in Nineveh demonstrated the mercy of God. Like many, Jonah in his zeal to discount the enemies in Nineveh had forgotten how indebted he was to God for the mercies He had already provided—the protection and deliverance by the miracle of a giant fish.

Sometimes we believe we can govern God's world better than God. The essence of receiving mercy is that we recognize and have reliance upon a power greater than ourselves. Such was the case with both Jeff and Jonah. They recognized the infinite, tender mercies of our God. We experience His mercy by receiving the goodness of God that confronts human suffering and guilt. It is an overwhelming vastness of divine pity and compassion.

There are several principles we can adapt in our lives to better understand and appreciate the mercy that typifies our heavenly Father.

God Shows Mercy on People with Bad Reputations

We often hear that God hates the sin but loves the sinner. A sincere love, compassion and goodness encompass God's character.

Even people with bad reputations are precious to God. God has always throttled His anger and disappointment with mankind because of His tender mercies.

Are you disappointed with yourself? Do you feel you have a poor reputation? Do not fear because our God is a loving, forgiving and merciful Father who wants you to know Him in a personal way. If you are truly repentant for your actions, attitudes and thoughts, He will immediately forgive and forget. It is the nature of His character and the gift of mercy.

"For the LORD your God is a merciful God; he will not abandon or destroy you or forget the covenant with your forefathers, which he confirmed to them by oath" (Deuteronomy 4:31).

God Hears The Call of Folks in Distress

The shortest prayer in the Bible is "Lord, save us" (Matthew 8:25). Whatever your distress, challenge, threat, or fear, God hears your prayer. He recognizes your plight and wants you to know that He is in control. Whatever the outcome, you can rest assured that He is sovereign and compassionate.

God heard Jonah call from within the giant fish, He heard Jeff's prayer in the brush tunnel, and He clearly hears our call. God wants to be our comforter and companion through those scary "brush tunnels of life." "Shout for joy, O heavens; rejoice, O earth; burst into song, O mountains! For the LORD comforts his people and will have compassion on his afflicted ones" (Isaiah 49:13).

God in His Compassion Turns Away from Judgment When People Are Truly Repentant

There will be a final judgment day for every person. The repentant Ninevites are an example of what it means to believe in God. The fasting and sackcloth indicate profound repentance. Through faith, all God's children can have fellowship with God.

As we live a repentant life, God provides a great deal of compassion and guidance if we are willing to listen. Jeff and Jonah were willing to listen and hear God's word in their lives.

God Expects Us to Mirror His Compassion

Once we understand the character of God and the traits that make up that nature, then we are asked to mimic those attributes. We are to be disciples of the Master. The word "disciple" means learner, pupil or student. Being disciples means following our Master by attitude and resulting action. The apostle James reminds us, "Prove yourself doers of the word, and not merely hearers who delude themselves" (James 1:22 NASB).

When you confront others who may not deserve your love or forgiveness, are you willing to show the kind of mercy God showed Jonah and the Ninevites?

God also showed mercy to Noah, Abraham and David. He has shown much mercy to guys like Jeff and me. He will continue to show mercy to His creation because it is part of His character.

"Blessed are the merciful, for they will be shown mercy" (Matthew 5:7).

Jesus commanded us to show mercy to others. Are we doing it?

Personal Application

- What does it mean to "be still and know that I am God"? (Psalm 46:10; see also Psalm 23).

- Where is your refuge or hiding place?

- What does it mean to show mercy?

- What was Paul trying to tell the church in Rome about God's mercy? (Romans 11).

Chapter 6

Alone in the Woods

God the Father

Have you ever been lost? It can be a scary feeling, particularly if you are in a potentially hostile environment without anyone around to help you find your way. The feelings of helplessness, isolation and uncertainty can grip your soul. Your heart begins to pound as you realize you might be lost. Sweat beads up on your forehead as you try to remember which way to go.

Your soul cries out: "I want my daddy!"

It is particularly challenging to keep a good orientation when you are in unfamiliar areas, heavily forested lands, desolate prairies, or snow-laden territories.

I remember the fear that overwhelmed me when I got lost in a department store at the age of five years. Then when I was eleven I went to an unfamiliar store a few blocks from my uncle's shop and got lost trying to get back. I think those early childhood traumas etched into my mind the importance of knowing where you are, where you are going and how to rely on someone with a better perspective than yours.

In preparing for this chapter I surveyed scores of hunting books and magazine articles. Not one of them mentioned anything about the problems associated with finding your way in the woods, getting lost or how to survive once you are lost. The only easily accessible information I could find on this topic came from the Internet. One of the best sources for detailed information on this subject is the Website "Equipped to Survive" at <u>www.equipped.org.</u>

I rarely hear anyone talk about their disorientation in the woods or on a prairie, yet the evening news reports regularly speak of individuals getting lost. It makes you wonder why folks don't talk about this fear.

Why Do We Get Lost?

Most often folks lose their way on hunting trips because they simply aren't paying attention and aren't taking the necessary precautions to identify where their base camp is. These folks are usually unprepared and hope that their innate sense of direction (luck) will help them find their way back. Unfortunately, our built-in guidance system gets off track when the thick woods block out where the sun is, when the snow-covered trees all begin to look alike, when a heavy rain or snowfall covers our trail or markers, when our pursuit of the quarry takes our focus off our navigation, when we fail to bring along some basic orienteering equipment, or when we lose track of the time of day or distance we traveled.

Help! I'm Lost

I highly recommend that anyone desiring to journey into unfamiliar terrain take a course on orienteering, read a good book on the subject or spend some time in the woods with seasoned outdoorsmen. In addition, I recommend accessing one of the many Web sites that help outdoorsmen get a handle on orienteering and survival in the outdoors.

One of the objectives of this book is to help encourage folks to develop a better understanding of specific outdoor skills and hunting strategies that will help improve their abilities. I don't consider myself an expert in the field of navigation or orienteering, but I am a prepared individual who uses a variety of systems to help keep me from getting lost—or, if I get lost, to help me survive the ordeal.

Orienteering and survival skills are important to the ultimate success and safety of any trip. The following is a partial list of various orienteering and survival items with a brief explanation of how they can help you be better prepared for venturing into unknown areas. If by some chance you get lost, these items may help you get home safely—or help you get out.

Compass—This simple device will aid any person in locating prominent landmarks that can help you triangulate your position. Used with a good topographic map, it should help you find your position most of the time.

Topographic Map—Take time to carefully study a detailed map of the area you will be hunting. It will not only give you a clue on where you might find game but also help you locate geographical features that can guide you to a specific location.

Global Positioning System (GPS)—There are many high-tech, low-cost electronic devices that interact with dozens of positioning satellites that will precisely guide a hunter to exact locations.

Survey Tape—Brightly colored survey tape used every 75-100 yards to mark trees or large bushes on the way into dense woods can help you find your way back home.

Two-Way Radios—The new ultralight radios can be helpful to hunters as they discuss their positions.

Whistles—The whistle is a vastly underrated signaling device. A whistle is far superior to shouting. Most whistles will carry for half a mile to two miles; your voice may only carry a few hundred yards.

Cellular Phones—The lightweight phones with long-range capability provide the possibility of reaching some remote microwave stations.

Signal Mirrors—Signaling mirrors are compact and simple to operate. They can help communicate your position or a message to others.

Chemical Luminescent Attractions—The new "snap light" light sticks provide a twelve-hour glow and good portability.

Battery-Powered Attraction—A strobe light is effective at night and can be seen up to five miles away.

So You're Lost—Now What?

STOP! Now is not the time for panic. Right now, you're in no danger. You may not know exactly where you are, but misplacing yourself is only a problem if you allow it to become one. Even the most experienced woodsman has found himself disoriented on occasion; it is nothing to be embarrassed about. The difference is that he knows it is not a serious problem yet, and it won't become one because he is prepared with knowledge and some basic tools. Now you won't have to worry, either, because we're going to teach you how to survive an unexpected stay in the wilderness.

There are innumerable ways you might end up in a wilderness survival situation, often through no fault of your own. How well things go will be determined by how prepared you are. Some basic survival knowledge can turn being lost into little more than an impromptu camping trip.

In almost any emergency, but especially in a survival situation, it is critical that you first S.T.O.P.

S is for **Stop.** Take a deep breath, sit down if possible, calm yourself, and recognize that whatever has happened to get you here is past and cannot be undone. You are now in a survival situation, and that means . . .

T is for **Think**. Your most important asset is your brain. Use it! Don't panic! Move with deliberate care. Think first so you have no regrets later. Take no action, even a footstep, until you have thought it through. Irreversible mistakes and injuries, potentially serious in a survival situation, occur when we act before we engage our brain. Then ...

O is for **Observe**. Take a look around you. Assess your situation and options. Consider the terrain, weather, and resources. Take stock of your supplies, equipment, surroundings, your personal capabilities, and the abilities of your fellow survivors, if there are any.

P is for **Plan**. Prioritize your immediate needs and develop a plan to systematically deal with the emergency and contingencies while conserving your energy. Then, follow your plan. Adjust your plan only as necessary to deal with changing circumstances.[1]

YOU WILL SURVIVE!

I Want My Daddy!

As a child, when I became lost, all I wanted was my daddy. I wanted to know my protector, comforter, encourager and provider was close at hand. I don't think it is any different today. When folks get lost they desire to know that someone is watching over them, guiding their every step and comforting their fears.

I think people who have gotten lost don't want to talk about their experiences because they might be perceived as incompetent or childish if they were to admit that they occasionally get confused about directions. Men are infamous for being self-reliant when it comes to these things. Perhaps that is why we will drive around in circles for hours looking for something without stopping to ask someone for directions.

Are we really ever alone in the woods? There are times when fearful and terrifying situations occur that remind us that our personal survival skills and the grace of God may be the only thing keeping us from experiencing a negative outcome. I have experienced hunting trips when I haven't seen a critter all day long. There are times after a snowstorm when the peace and solitude one feels in the quietness of the moment cause a person to wonder if they may be the only person on earth. As we have already seen through other stories, we are never really alone—God is ever-present.

I have come across people wandering through the woods who are looking for game but are still focused on their problems. People frequently journey to the woods to find solace and peace. They are looking for a way to comfort their fears, still their anger, and relieve their despondency. They are trying to quiet the personal storms of life.

Some folks talk to the forest as they would to their caring Father. They beckon the trees to wrap their mighty limbs around their shaken frames. Unfortunately, their pleas go unanswered because they are speaking to the creation rather than the Creator. Out of the depths of their souls these lost individuals cry out: "HELP ME!" Without God, nature turns a deaf ear to their unbelieving hearts and appeals. Only God the Father can provide the comfort and encouragement that is needed. He hears our cries. "The eyes of the LORD are toward the righteous, and His ears are open to their cry" (Psalm 34:15 NASB).

He Is the Alpha and Omega

Scripture gives us much insight on God the Father. He is the ALPHA and OMEGA. This title is given to God the Father and God the Son (Revelation 1:8; 21:6). The risen Christ says, "I am the Alpha and the Omega, the Beginning and the End, the First and the Last" (Revelation 22:13 NKJV). By calling Jesus

Christ the Alpha and the Omega, the writer of the book of Revelation acknowledges that He is the Creator, the Redeemer, and the Final Judge of all things.[2]

Jesus reaffirmed to the children of Israel what their Scriptures taught and what faithful, godly Jews had always believed: God is the Father ... in heaven of those who trust in Him. He used the title Father in all of His prayers except the one He prayed on the cross, when He cried "My God, my God" (Matthew 27:46), which emphasized the separation He experienced in bearing mankind's sin. Though the text uses the Greek *Patér*, it is likely that Jesus used the Aramaic *Abba* when He said this prayer. Not only was Aramaic the language in which He and most other Palestinian Jews commonly spoke; *Abba* (equivalent to our "Daddy") also carried a more intimate and personal connotation than *Patér*. In a number of passages the term *Abba* is used even in the Greek text, and is usually simply transliterated in English versions (see Mark 14:36; Romans 8:15; Galatians 4:6).[3]

Knowing Our Father

In his book *Knowing God as Father*, James Robison dedicates the work to "those who have had no father, who have had absent fathers or fathers unable to fulfill their role in the family, and those who have been blessed with good fathers— in the hope that, through this book, the reader might enter into a joyful, personal relationship with the ultimate and eternal Father."[4]

Life was particularly tough for James Robison's mother Myra. She was a hard-working practical nurse who was renting a room from a family in Houston, Texas. One evening after a very difficult day, the owner's son forced his way into her room and raped her. The forty-one-year-old woman decided the best way to end this unwanted pregnancy was to abort the fetus. After consulting with a few physicians, she was persuaded to give birth to the child and offer him up for adoption. She put an ad in the paper, and the Reverend and Mrs. Hale of Pasadena, Texas, promptly answered. They picked up James and reared him with love and care until he was five. His mother wouldn't give final custody to the Hales and had James brought back to live with her. Unfortunately, she had little to offer him except more grief and frustration. They lived in a very poor neighborhood where bullies regularly preyed upon James.[5]

Robison writes that he experienced a sad, miserable childhood: "At the time I was so despondent, felt so worthless, that many nights I cried and cried. I figured I was a bad boy, and that must be why I never got any breaks. No dad. No friends. No sports to play. No loved ones who remembered me. Sometimes, when I was home alone, I banged my head against the wall until I knocked myself out. I just wanted to escape."[6]

Divine Help

James recalls his feelings during his childhood: "Without a father growing up, there were precious few people who wanted to take a disenfranchised boy out fishing or hunting. As my relationship grew with God I realized he was the father I never had. He cares about what I care about. He likes to see me have fun. I regularly called upon him for help in finding fish and deer. God certainly knew what area of the lake to send Peter (Matthew 17) and what side of the boat to tell the disciples to throw their nets (John 21:6) and how to direct David to kill a lion and bear.

"When I was a little boy, I especially wanted a dad to take me fishing or hunting. Sometimes I would just sit outside and imagine I was having a good time enjoying God's creation. I now tell people everywhere I go that my Father, God, takes me fishing or hunting. And He knows where the game is! Of course, those in the audience smile and many laugh. But then

I often quickly add that, although He knows where they are, He won't always tell me! He likes to watch me look for them. And yes, my Father in Heaven enjoys my excitement when I do, in fact, get a big one!"[7]

Many times Robison was saved from near death by the intervening hand of God, but amid the negatives, a few positive memories shine through. He writes fondly of his first exposure to nature:"Today I am a hunter and a conservationist because Timbo (a onetime housemate) took the time to take me into the woods as a little boy. Somehow, she knew it was in me to want to spend time in the great outdoors. Hunting and fishing with her provided some of the most pleasant experiences of my childhood."[8]

He talks about praying that his own desires would never get in the way of God's will for his life, pleading with the Lord never to let him lose his love for God, to use him in a mighty way, to remind him of his promise to always come back to God in private where it was just Robison and the Lord, loving each other. (It seems that this is a key to perseverance—coming beside restful waters and lying down in green pastures with the Lord to be refreshed and loved by Him.)

God Is the Father to the Lost

Since God is a Person, He can enter into personal relationships—and the closest and tenderest is that of Father. Regardless of our background, environment, failures or successes, each of us has a deep and very personal need for a father. God our Father is the only perfect and effective Father I know. He is all-knowing, all-comforting, all-caring, all-sufficient, all-powerful and all-holy. He is the Almighty One who desires an intimate relationship with each of us.

Jesus often referred to God as Father. As He taught the disciples to pray, Jesus told them, "But when you pray, go into your room, close the door and pray to your Father, who is unseen. Then your Father, who sees what is done in secret, will reward you. And when you pray, do not keep on babbling like pagans, for they think they will be heard because of their many words. Do not be like them, for your Father knows what you need before you ask him. This, then, is how you should pray: Our Father in heaven, hallowed be your name..." (Matthew 6:6-9). Christ's relationship with God the Father was at the deepest level.

Knowing His fate on Calvary's cross, Jesus cried out: "*Abba*, Father...everything is possible for you. Take this cup from me. Yet not what I will, but what you will" (Mark 14:36).

The apostle Paul also had a deep and abiding relationship with God the Father. Throughout his missionary journeys, he called out to God in the most intimate of language. He called on God as a young lad would his daddy: "Abba Father." "For you did not receive a spirit that makes you a slave again to fear, but you received the Spirit of sonship. And by Him we cry, 'Abba, Father' " (Romans 8:15).

Malachi, the Old Testament prophet, in calling his people to faithfulness to God and to consideration for one another, asks: "Have we not all one Father? Has not one God created us?" (Malachi 2:10 NKJV).

And the prophet Isaiah pleads to God for mercy: "But now, O LORD, thou art our father; we are the clay, and thou our potter; we all are the work of thy hand" (Isaiah 64:8 KJV).

Four Ways to Know God the Father

A woodsman can know God in the most fundamental way through His great creation. The **Father of Creation** bestows the gift of life. Every living thing we enjoy is attributed to the fatherhood of God. The animals that impress us with their elusive nature, the trees we hide between to escape detection from our quarry, and even the very ground we all rest upon was made by a loving and creative God.

Most importantly, mankind has been created in God's image. "So God created man in his own image, in the image of God he created him; male and female he created them" (Genesis 1:27). Without the Father of Creation there would be no race of man, no family of mankind and certainly no gift of life.[9]

The second attribute of the fatherhood of God is revealed in His covenant with Israel. **The Father of a Nation** has established a collective relationship with those who follow His teachings and are obedient in their worship. This of course extends to the New Testament church—those who follow Christ Jesus. Believers who really know God experience His infinite peace, comfort and joy. Like a good worldly father, God wants to love His children in a very tangible way.

"The man who says, 'I know him' but does not do what he commands is a liar, and the truth is not in him. But if anyone obeys his word, God's love is truly made complete in him. This is how we know we are in him: Whoever claims to live in him must walk as Jesus did" (1 John 2:4-6).

This Scripture leads us right into the third way we see the fatherhood of God. When Jesus claimed and proved to be the Son of God it showed that God is **The Father of a Savior.** The second Person of the Trinity is designated as the Son of God, the only begotten Son. Christ frequently spoke of His relationship to the Almighty who was His Father by eternal generation. This timeless relationship transcends our comprehension.[10]

In the gospel of John, Jesus reminds all of us that by believing in Him we share in the inheritance: "Do not hold on to me, for I have not yet returned to the Father. Go instead to my brothers and tell them, 'I am returning to my Father and your Father, to my God and your God'" (John 20:17).

The final trait associated with the fatherhood of God is seen through His adoptive nature.

When the apostle Paul reminded the believers in Galatia, "You are all sons of God through faith in Christ

Jesus" (Galatians 3:26), He was speaking about knowing God as **The Father of Adoption.** Through our relationship to Jesus Christ, by believing in His redemptive powers, we are adopted into the family of God. The precious blood that Jesus shed on Calvary's cross entitled His followers to be justified and cleansed of their sins so they could be born (adopted) into a divine relationship with the Father.

This relationship of adoption is restricted to "believing people." The apostle John made it clear in the initial pages of his gospel: "Yet to all who received him, to those who believed in his name, he gave the right to become *children of God*—children born not of natural descent, nor of human decision or a husband's will, but born of God" (John 1:12-13, emphasis added).

James Robison helps us get a handle on the above verse: "To become your Father, God first had to deal with the legal problem brought on by the sin in your life…you deserved the spiritual death penalty for your sins. Humanly speaking, there was no way you could avoid this penalty. You couldn't pay it—except by death. And, since 'all have sinned,' no one else could pay it for you. Redemption means Christ paid the price for us to be set free from the death sentence we had received for our sins." [11]

As you would expect of a father, God is loving, kind, compassionate, tender, forgiving and sensitive to His children. As loving children we have the responsibility to trust, obey and worship God as we show our reverence and humility.

James Robison was a young boy without an earthly father to encourage and support him during those important formative years. While he missed that relationship, he was able to discover an even more important relationship with a Father who infinitely cares for and loves His creation. The next time you wander in the woods, stop to listen and feel His presence. If you haven't already asked Him to become your eternal Father, affirm the relationship with this simple prayer:

"Almighty God, I know I have failed and need the love, care and compassion that only You can provide. The sins of my life haunt me like a scarlet blood trail on fresh fallen snow. I ask You to forgive me of my sins and help me find a new direction and purpose in life. I want You in my life as my 'Abba Father.' Through the redeeming power of the cleansing blood of Your Son Jesus, may You welcome me into Your family and allow me to have a deep and personal relationship with You. AMEN."

Personal Application

- How does a person receive God as Father?

  Read Romans 10:9,10,13; Ephesians 2:8,9

- Knowing God as our Father settles the matter of loneliness. How do John 14:21 and Psalm 68:5,6 speak to your heart about the issue of loneliness?

- What does it mean to be part of the family?

  Read Ephesians 2:19

- What do the following verses say about Jesus as your brother?

  Read Hebrews 2:11-13,17; Romans 8:29; Colossians 1:18

- If you are now in God's family, what does it mean to have close family fellowship?

  Read Romans 12:10-13

Chapter 7

The Love of a Father

God Is Love

We continue to fill our spiritual survival packs with an understanding of God's character. There is no more fundamental survival need than the need to experience God's love and the love of others. There are those who come from abusive backgrounds where real love and appreciation were not demonstrated. These folks may have difficulty feeling loved or displaying affection to others.

The fact that God's very nature is to love may be a foreign concept to explore. To say you believe in God is to accept His very nature and character, which includes an infinite ability to love His creation. God's love is often demonstrated through those who love the most. Such was the case with a young hunter named Jim Dobson.

While he was attending a pediatric conference at his hotel in San Antonio, Texas, in September 1977, Dr. James Dobson received a call from Dr. Paul Cunningham, his father's physician. The deafening words "heart attack" were used to describe his father's condition. The following morning Dr. Cunningham again called Jim to update him. The news was not good; his father's condition had worsened.

Jim and his wife, Shirley, quickly made their way across the country to the bedside of Jim's dying father. Throughout the prolonged plane trip to Kansas, a kaleidoscope of memories flooded Jim's mind. His thoughts returned to some of the happiest days of his life, occurring between ten and thirteen years of age.

Upon arrival Jim and Shirley were ushered into his dad's critical-care room. As Jim looked down at his loving dad, he reflected upon the times of inspiration and the lessons taught during some of their outdoor excursions.

He recalled the times his dad would wake him up very early, before the sun came up, on wintry mornings. They would put on hunting clothes and heavy boots and drive twenty miles from the little town where they lived. After unpacking the car and climbing over a fence, they would enter a wooded area they called the "big woods" because the trees seemed so large to both of them. They would slip down to the creek bed and follow the winding stream several miles back into the forest.

Jim's dad would hide him under a fallen tree that made a little room with its branches. Then he would find a similar shelter for himself around a bend in the creek. There they would wait for the arrival of the sun and the awakening of the animal world. Little squirrels and birds and chipmunks would scurry back and forth, not knowing they were being observed. The two hunters would watch as the breathtaking panorama of the morning unfolded. It spoke eloquently of the God who made all things.

There was something dramatic that occurred out there in the forest between father and son. Intense love and affection were generated on those mornings that set the tone for a lifetime of fellowship. There was a closeness, a oneness, that made Jim want to be like his father…that made him choose his father's values as his values, his dad's dreams as his dreams, the God known and loved by his hero as his God.

On December 4, 1977, Jim Dobson's father suffered a massive heart attack and died. Jim lost not only his father but a real friend.[1]

Memories formed in God's great outdoors are not easily lost, and they form immeasurable bonds between people. Some of life's most important lessons are taught to people during moments of leisure time. When it comes to loving others, we find that there is no substitute for practical evidences of our affection.

We should never underestimate the power of unstructured environments. Free of the stress barriers and emotional obstacles that surround some institutional environments the outdoors often presents spontaneous opportunities for sharing our cares, teaching principles, and modeling values.

Gordon MacDonald said, "Family Life is an existential classroom; it lasts for about eighteen years." Our children are daily molded and shaped by the interaction with their peer group, societal pressures, media, life experiences, and, most important, the nurturing communications of loving fathers. Each day a committed father has an opportunity to etch into the lives of his children attitudes, words, habits, and reactions that will shape their personality and behavior.

Most youth have developed sensitivities and erected barriers of apprehension that can at times stifle effective communication with their parents. By using those invaluable leisure times as opportunities to invest in the lives of children, parents can be seen in a more natural setting where friendships and trust can evolve.

The casual nature of outdoor environments also provides a unique teaching and training atmosphere that encourages exploration and creativity. While dad is teaching exciting leisure skills, he is helping build the child's self-esteem by delegating responsibilities and supporting inventiveness.

Every experience in family life can be a teaching opportunity. Squeezing worms onto a hook, setting traps in the woods, cuddling up in a blind patiently waiting for the deer to appear, these are cherished times. Enduring love, lasting memories, and deep trust are built through these pacesetting experiences. Remember, no day is ever wasted in the life of an effective father.

Abba Father—God Is Love

When the apostle John, by the Spirit, wrote, "God is love" (see 1 John 4:8), he did not intend to suggest that this was the only attribute that characterizes God. If God literally is love, and nothing else, then we must infer that love is God. But they are not interchangeable. We are directed to worship God, not love.

The words "God is love" mean that love is an essential attribute of God. Love is something true of God, but it is not all there is to God. It expresses the way God is in His character. Love permeates the Father and undergirds His being. It is important to remember that we do not want to worship love but Him who is love. If we worship love, then we risk becoming idolaters.

It is through the knowledge of God's other attributes that we can fully appreciate how much He loves us. We know that because He is self-existent and eternal, His love has no beginning or end. God is infinite, having no limits; therefore, His love is boundless in form. The holiness of God suggests that His love is pure and undefiled in any way.

Love wills goodness. When we are affected with love for another person, we search for the goodness in their lives. Love emphasizes the positives and de-emphasizes the negatives. Because of God's great love, He forgets our sinful acts and rejoices in our good works. The Psalmist writes: "Remember not the sins of my youth and my rebellious ways; according to your love remember me, for you are good, O LORD" (Psalm 25:7).

- According to the apostle John, love is the opposite of fear: "There is no fear in love; but perfect love casteth out fear" (1 John 4:18 KJV). When the young Jim Dobson was tucked in the blind awaiting a chance at a nice buck, he knew of his dad's great love and care, which brought about feelings of comfort and peace. Likewise, we can expect that same sense of security when we allow ourselves to experience God's love.

To know that love is of God and to enter into the embrace of His Spirit brings about tranquility even in the presence of potentially fearful situations. Martin Luther once wrote in the great hymn of faith "A Mighty Fortress Is Our God," "The body they may kill: God's truth abideth still, His kingdom is forever."

- Love is also an emotional identification. Jim Dobson saw his dad sacrifice time and resources to make the day in the woods special for him. Acts of self-sacrifice are common in those who love. When a father places his son in a favorable shooting spot so that he can circle around the area to help direct the game to the ambush spot—this is sacrifice and love.

When we look at the character of God, we see an even greater sacrifice: His only begotten Son. Christ speaking to His followers described it this way: "Greater love hath no man than this, that a man lay down his life for his friends" (John 15:13 KJV).

- Though God is self-sufficient, He has allowed His heart to be emotionally identified with a needy creation. He wants our love and desires a relationship with each of us. "Herein is love, not that we loved God, but that he loved us, and sent his Son to be the propitiation [sacrifice] for our sins" (1 John 4:10 KJV).

Self-sufficient as He is, God desires our love. He has allowed His heart to be bonded with mankind and desires a loving relationship with His creation. He placed within the heart and spirit of man the capacity to show affection. However, God's love is not conditional; it is not based on our ability to love Him.

Another characteristic of God's love is that He takes pleasure in His creation. As Jim Dobson's father looked across the field with great pleasure at his loving son snuggled in the deer blind, so, too, does God look down upon the works of His creation with great delight. God is happy in His love for all He has made—He has deemed it "very good" (Genesis 1:31).

The inspired Psalmist gives us a glimpse into God's mind and reveals His pleasure with His creation:

Praise the LORD, O my soul.
O LORD my God, you are very great;
you are clothed with splendor and majesty.
He wraps himself in light as with a garment;
he stretches out the heavens like a tent
and lays the beams of his upper chambers on their waters.
He makes the clouds his chariot
and rides on the wings of the wind.
He makes winds his messengers,
flames of fire his servants.
He set the earth on its foundations;
it can never be moved.
You covered it with the deep as with a garment;
the waters stood above the mountains.
But at your rebuke the waters fled,
at the sound of your thunder they took to flight;
they flowed over the mountains,
they went down into the valleys,
to the place you assigned for them.
You set a boundary they cannot cross;

never again will they cover the earth.
He makes springs pour water into the ravines;
it flows between the mountains.
They give water to all the beasts of the field;
the wild donkeys quench their thirst.
The birds of the air nest by the waters;
they sing among the branches.
He waters the mountains from his upper chambers;
the earth is satisfied by the fruit of his work.
He makes grass grow for the cattle,
and plants for man to cultivate—
bringing forth food from the earth:
wine that gladdens the heart of man,
oil to make his face shine,
and bread that sustains his heart.
The trees of the LORD are well watered,
the cedars of Lebanon that he planted.
There the birds make their nests;
the stork has its home in the pine trees.
The high mountains belong to the wild goats;
the crags are a refuge for the coneys.
The moon marks off the seasons,
and the sun knows when to go down.
You bring darkness, it becomes night,
and all the beasts of the forest prowl.
The lions roar for their prey
and seek their food from God.
The sun rises, and they steal away;
they return and lie down in their dens.
Then man goes out to his work,
to his labor until evening.
How many are your works, O LORD!
In wisdom you made them all;
the earth is full of your creatures.
There is the sea, vast and spacious,

teeming with creatures beyond number—
living things both large and small.
There the ships go to and fro,
and the leviathan, which you formed to frolic there.
These all look to you
to give them their food at the proper time.
When you give it to them,
they gather it up;
when you open your hand,
they are satisfied with good things.
When you hide your face,
they are terrified;
when you take away their breath,
they die and return to the dust.
When you send your Spirit,
they are created,
and you renew the face of the earth.
May the glory of the LORD endure forever;
may the LORD rejoice in his works—
he who looks at the earth, and it trembles,
who touches the mountains, and they smoke.
I will sing to the LORD all my life;
I will sing praise to my God as long as I live.
May my meditation be pleasing to him,
as I rejoice in the LORD.
But may sinners vanish from the earth
and the wicked be no more.
Praise the LORD, O my soul.
Praise the LORD.

—Psalm 104:1-35

Finally, Scripture reminds us that all believing souls are objects of God's love. "The LORD thy God in the midst of thee is mighty; he will save, he will rejoice over thee with joy; he will rest in his love, he will joy over thee with singing" (Zephaniah 3:17 KJV).

The pleasure that is nearest to God is love. One of the purest ways to express this is through music. Heaven will be full of music because it is among the purest pleasures and joys God embraces. Hell, on the other hand, will not have any pleasures because there is an absence of God and love. These two elements cannot exist in an evil environment. And in an environment of hate and ill will, we can assume that no music will exist either.

One of the pillars of the Christian faith is believers' deep and abiding love of God and each other. If God is love, then we must demonstrate that love in a tangible way. Acts of good will, kindness, compassion and physical affection telegraph our willingness to identify with a Christlike character. Jesus said, "This is My commandment, that you love one another as I have loved you" (John 15:12 NKJV).

It is easy to say, "But you don't know my background and the terrible things that were done to me." And there are some who would not accept the concept of a loving God because of various catastrophes. My friend, let me assure you that the character of God is not affected by a sinful world that has ignored His principles for mankind to live in love and harmony.

To the contrary, it is rare to see someone involved in deviant behavior if his or her family experience involved a Christlike love. Folks who are involved in destructive behavior most likely have not embraced or accepted God's love. "Whoever does not love does not know God, because God is love" (1 John 4:8).

We see evidence of love all around us. Certainly our story about Jim Dobson's father is an example of how human love can manifest itself. Did you know that God's love is so great that He cannot divorce Himself from those who have accepted Him as Savior, Lord and Creator? The Jewish law tells us that an adopted child has more rights and entitlements than a natural-born child. This principle of God's love can be seen in Scripture as testified to by the apostle John: "How great is the love the Father has lavished on us, that we should be called children of God! And that is what we are!" (1 John 3:1).

You ask, "How can I know such love?" Shortly after Christ's death, Saul of Tarsus, who had been persecuting Christians, found God's love through a series of events that took place on a road to Damascus. He went on to accept the Son of God as his personal Savior and then proclaim the love of God to thousands. In his second letter to the church in Corinth, Paul urges believers to cultivate Christ's love among them:

> *Finally, brothers.... Aim for perfection, listen to my appeal, be of one mind, live in peace. And the God of love and peace will be with you. Greet one another with a holy kiss. All the saints send their greetings. May the grace of the Lord Jesus Christ, and the love of God, and the fellowship of the Holy Spirit be with you all* (2 Corinthians 13:11-14).

And James reminds us that it is through prayer that we can find God and understand His deep and abiding love: "Draw near to God and He will draw near to you" (James 4:8 NKJV).

Personal Application

- Are you drawing near to God through Bible study, fellowship with believers, and prayer?

- Are you laying down your life (desires and selfish wants) to provide memories in the outdoors with your children?

- Will you let your heavenly Father provide shelter for you?

Chapter 8

Overcoming Obstacles

The Power of God

As mentioned earlier, God's attributes are not isolated or limited to our finite thoughts. As we experience various facets of His being, our understanding of the true Godhead is shaped and molded.

God possesses what no creature can: an incomprehensible capacity for power and might. I'm reminded of what the Psalmist says: "So great is your power" (Psalm 66:3).

God gives to His creation the ability to harness and utilize power. In a futile attempt to emulate God, man captures wind or water flow to drive huge turbines that create energy. We can split an atom so that it releases its force to be utilized in a variety of applications. But we cannot even begin to understand the awesomeness of His mighty power. Earthquakes, hurricanes and lightning storms reshape our earth daily. The dynamic energy that holds the universe together is but a mere glimpse of the power God wields to rule over His creation.

It is truly a wonder how He allows various animals to reign and defend their domain with great strength or speed. The animal kingdom is unique in its ability to consume foods and supplements that nourish and strengthen their bodies to achieve mighty works.

The knowledge and wisdom we humans have to effectively live life is limited to our finite capacity to understand the power of God. If we would simply take the time to evaluate the gifts God has given us, we could better appreciate the body/mind experience and its many implications to discerning God's limitless power.

A Record Bear

When a hunter thinks about power he most often will consider the North American brown bear. This powerful beast is well known for its protectiveness and great strength. In its twenty-five-year life span, it will often achieve a weight of 500-800 pounds.

Because of their size, speed, agility, strength, and nature, these creatures present the hunter with a formidable challenge. There is nothing in the woods that will cause a hunter's knees to shake more than an angry bear standing on its hind paws, popping its jaws with discontent at an intruding visitor.

Such was the case with my good friend Jim Otto and his hunting companion Jim Harvey. These All-Pro Oakland Raiders were at the height of their professional careers and in tremendous shape as they journeyed to Alaska for the hunt of a lifetime.

In the mid-seventies Jim Otto was recognized as the top center in football. His fifteen years of heroic play made him one of the most popular men to ever play the game. Otto, a sure-handed ball-snapper and a superior blocker who sought out targets far beyond the area normally expected of a center, was a perennial tower of strength and power, and a regular participant in the Pro Bowl games.

His election in his first year of eligibility to the Pro Football Hall of Fame in Canton, Ohio, in 1980 fulfilled a dream and culminated a lot of hard work. But this warrior of the gridiron, who has now undergone more than thirty-eight surgeries to repair damage suffered in the "trenches," would find that his greatest struggle would not be against an All-Pro linebacker but against a trophy brown bear.

During the off-season in 1974, Otto underwent a complicated knee surgery that included the implanting of an artificial right knee. After a little time for healing, this avid hunter knew it was time to try for his ultimate trophy—a giant Alaskan brown bear.

In late spring of 1974, the two Raiders found themselves landing on a small piece of tundra in the Aleutian Islands near Port Heiden, Alaska. The two Jims then met their guides, John Swiss and Bill Erickson.

The bears had come out of winter hibernation and were eating everything in sight. During the weeks preceding the hunt, the guides had spotted several big bears in the area. The two hunters said they didn't want "just any ole bear": they wanted a real trophy!

Bill was hesitant to share the information about his favorite big bear area near Black Lake. "I knew these guys wanted a good bear, but I also knew that it would take a major effort to find and kill such a beast under the present conditions," he says. They would have to walk fifteen miles on the snow-covered tundra just to get into the area—a great challenge for a fit person, let alone a man recovering from a knee operation.

The men weighed their options and decided to go for it. The hike into the area took all day. It was slow going because of the wet tundra and the heavy hip waders they wore to keep their feet dry. Jim recalls, "Every step was an effort as we navigated our way to the canyon area."

They surveyed a number of valleys as they continued to hunt for that ultimate bear. As they approached a ridge, Bill spotted a nice brown bear quietly feeding in a nearby meadow. The two Jims hustled up the steep hill and tried to find a steady position from which to try a shot.

It was Jim Otto's chance to size up this critter to see if it met his expectations. "I'm not sure that this is the guy," he said. "He is all bent over and does not really seem to be that big."

"You have to be kidding," Bill said. "That bear is a giant! You guys have been hanging out too long with big people and lost your ability to judge size anymore."

No sooner had Bill finished his remarks than the wind shifted and the great bear turned and peered at the hunters. His posture and behavior became more aggressive. It was now or never.

Jim lowered his 7 mm Parker and Hale rifle and peered through his scope. The small alder trees provided the perfect backdrop for the 280-yard shot. Jim squeezed the trigger as the 180-grain bullet found its mark. The fallen bear began to call out as Otto's rifle again barked. The second and finishing shot put the big bear down for good.

There were "high-fives" for the entire group as they danced around the ridge until Bill provided an observation. "Guys, we have about two hours of light left before we need to get headed back. We need to quickly skin out this animal and begin packing him back to base camp."

As they approached the bear, Otto's eyes began to bulge out of their sockets. The men stood over the bear with their mouths wide open. This bear was so big that even the guide was impressed. "Look at his front paw—it is as big as your chest, Jim!" Bill estimated the bear to be more than eleven feet tall and about 1,300 pounds.

With minimal rations and wearing sweat-soaked clothing, the weary hunters began skinning out the animal and making their way back to camp. After several attempts to have one man carry the hide and another the skull, they realized that the weight of the skin was too great for one guy. Bill figured that the cape weighed at least 250 pounds. The fast skinning job left some fat on the hide that produced an extra burden for the weary hunters.

They took a vinyl bag that held some of their dry clothing and loaded the skin and head onto the mat. By hooking up some rope to a small alder tree they had cut down, two men could pull the load through the ice and snow. "We felt like a team of plow horses pulling our load through the snow," Jim said. The long, exhausting day was not yet over.

Two hours into the "big pull," a fierce snowstorm developed, creating whiteout conditions. Shortly the men lost their bearings and were unable to figure out their pathway home. The sweat-laden warriors began to feel their body temperatures drop as the moisture in their clothes began to freeze. They decided to seek out a wind-protected area to huddle up and keep warm. The only way to regain strength would be to get some rest.

After laying a solar blanket on the snow, they placed the bear rug on the mat and wrapped themselves in the fur. But after a few hours' sleep, the initial stages of hypothermia were beginning to set in on Otto. He told his friends, "If I don't get up and move around, I will freeze to death. The storm has let up a little, so let's get packin'."

Once again, the men started their journey back to camp, but the power and strength of these great football players had been exhausted. Every step was a challenge as they realized their limits and the serious obstacles they faced. Prior to this hunt they felt that their awesome stamina and might would carry them through any situation; now they were unsure of their fate.

Finally, at 10:30 in the morning, these weary men stumbled into camp, exhausted and thankful to be alive. Jim recalls being so tired that after putting on some dry clothes he fell fast asleep on top of his bunk without even eating. About two hours into his sleep, Otto heard some shouting and yelling from the cabin next to his. "Otto wake up, man, wake up! You have a record bear, my friend."

Jim staggered into the hut to see his bear hide stretched out on the floor. The measuring tape showed this bear to be a record eleven-foot-six monster.

After the celebration, Jim retired again to his quiet cabin, where he reflected upon the adventure and the awesomeness of God. He thought about the grandeur of the breathtaking scenery they had experienced. "Only a powerful and mighty God could have created such a wonderful display of beauty," he says. Jim also realized his own limitations when compared to the power of God. Despite the fact that he and his partner were among the most physically fit individuals in this country, their abilities and strength paled in comparison to the mighty power God displayed through the snowstorm.

God's Power over Our Circumstances

Jim Otto is a firm believer in relying on God's power (His omnipotence) to help control any circumstance. He has witnessed it throughout his life and professional career. He has also seen it many times amplified in Scripture.

One of my favorite Bible stories—one that will help us better understand how we can use God's power in our lives— comes during a critical period in the development of Israel and Judah. Mount Carmel was the setting that God used to display His strength and power to exhort the children of Israel to worship. The primary principle God was teaching through this incident was the importance of His chosen people to fully commit and dedicate themselves to the Mosaic covenant.

We pick up on the history of various kings about 600 years before Christ. In 1 Kings 18 we see the power of God demonstrated in a very tangible way to help the nation of Israel return to His covenants.

King Ahab, the son of King Omri, did evil in the sight of the Lord. His sin was greater than all the kings who had preceded him. He had set an altar to Baal, the Canaanite storm god who supposedly provided the rain necessary for the fertility of the land. The worship of Baal had infiltrated Israel long before the time of Ahab. But King Ahab gave it official sanction and built a temple to encourage people to worship this god rather than God Almighty, the great I AM. Idolatry and gross immorality became the order of the day.

A prophet of God named Elijah came on the scene and realized the importance of encouraging folks to return to their worship of the true God of Abraham and Isaac. Elijah prayed to God that no dew or rain would touch the land for three years as a way to humble the idolaters. The drought would prove that Baal, the god of the rains and fertility, was impotent before the power of God Almighty.

Finally King Ahab could not stand it anymore and asked Elijah to present himself. The famine in the land was great, and the king was desperate and frustrated. He saw Elijah as a real troublemaker.

"I have not made trouble for Israel," Elijah replied. "But you and your father's family have. You have abandoned the LORD's commands and have followed the Baals" (1 Kings 18:18).

At their meeting it was agreed that all the prophets of Baal, the prophets of Asherah (wife of a Canaanite god), and all the Israelites would be invited to witness a showdown between King Ahab and Elijah. More than a contest between these two men, it was a contest between the God of all mankind and the false gods of the idolaters.

Elijah asked the assembled group a profound question that men still struggle with today: "How long will you waver between two opinions? If the LORD is God, follow him; but if Baal is God, follow him" (1 Kings 18:21). It appears the crowd could not choose, and their lack of devotion and commitment created the perfect environment for God to display His mighty power.

Power Through Miracles

"Then Elijah said to them, 'I am the only one of the LORD's prophets left, but Baal has four hundred and fifty prophets. Get two bulls for us. Let them choose one for themselves, and let them cut it into pieces and put it on the wood but not set fire to it. I will prepare the other bull and put it on the wood but not set fire to it. Then you call on the name of your god, and I will call on the name of the LORD. The god who answers by fire—he is God.' "

"Then all the people said, 'What you say is good.' " (1 Kings 18:22–24). "In modern-day language they were saying, "Let's have a Super Bowl between the gods.""

The prophets of Baal prepared the bull and called upon their gods to put fire under the altar, but there was no response. Elijah continued to urge them to call out to their gods that their power might be displayed for all to see. In desperation, the false prophets cut themselves as a token of their allegiance and personal sacrifice, hoping that their gods would show pity and respond with the fire.

Elijah was so positive of God's faithfulness and power that he didn't want anyone to think that trickery would be involved with the fire in his pit. He asked the servants to dump twelve buckets of water on the wood. There was so much water that even the blood trench around the altars was flooded.

As testified to in God's Word, an awesome display of God's power and Elijah's faithfulness came forth.

"At the time of sacrifice, the prophet Elijah stepped forward and prayed: 'O LORD, God of Abraham, Isaac and Israel, let it be known today that you are God in Israel and that I am your servant and have done all these things at your command.

Answer me, O LORD, answer me, so these people will know that you, O LORD, are God, and that you are turning their hearts back again.'

"Then the fire of the LORD fell and burned up the sacrifice, the wood, the stones and the soil, and also licked up the water in the trench. When all the people saw this, they fell prostrate and cried, 'The LORD—he is God! The LORD—he is God!'

"Then Elijah commanded them, 'Seize the prophets of Baal. Don't let anyone get away!'

"They seized them, and Elijah had them brought down to the Kishon Valley and slaughtered there" (1 Kings 18:36-40).

The drought ended, and once again the Israelites bowed to the presence and power of God in their lives.

What are the lessons we can take from this test?

Lessons Learned from a Football Player and a Fire

The prophets of Baal had failed in their proof, and could give no evidence at all of their pretensions on behalf of their gods. Elijah had, by the most convincing and undeniable evidence, proved his claims on behalf of the God of Israel.

The people, as the jury, gave their verdict in the trial, and they are all agreed in it; the case was so plain that they didn't need to go from the mountain to consider their verdict or consult about it. They fell on their faces and claimed, "Jehovah, He is the God, and not Baal. We are convinced and satisfied of it. Jehovah, He is the God" (see 1 Kings 18:39). You would think that they would have listened to their forefathers who said, "We will serve the LORD our God and obey him" (Joshua 24:24).

Like Elijah and Jim Otto, other faithful servants of God have become shortsighted and filled with fear. When our faith in God's power is gone, we lose our confidence and run from that which really shouldn't intimidate us. If we allow them, challenges and obstacles can paralyze us with fright and prevent us from proclaiming God's truth.

Read Matthew 10:24–33. What did Jesus tell His disciples? If you have an antagonistic co-worker, neighbor, or relative, pray that God will give you boldness to speak the truth in love.

Blessings Through God's Power

God Is Everything

Jim Otto's fame, fortune and success were not going to get him out of his predicament. There was no magic skyhook to remove him from the situation he faced. It was only his sheer determination and faith in the power of God over the problem that allowed Jim to continue.

King David, in one of his psalms of praise, stated it this way: "Wealth and honor come from you; you are the ruler of all things. In your hands are strength and power to exalt and give strength to all" (1 Chronicles 29:12).

God Is Our Rescuer

Jim Otto's faith in God proved to be the internal strength that fueled his drive to not give up. The storms of life will often attack us, as did the biting cold of the Alaskan territory grip Jim Otto's body. But God wants us to persevere and continue the fight to the finish. God rescues us with His strength and power if we have asked the Holy Spirit into our lives. He wants us to rest in Him and depend on Him for the wisdom, stamina, and power to conquer the obstacles before us—"So that your faith might not rest on men's wisdom, but on God's power" (1 Corinthians 2:5).

God Is Our Shield

When Jim needed comforting, he found a sheltered area and a thick bear hide to shield him against the fury of the storm. In a similar manner, God wants to be our shield and comforter. We are kept by His power; a supreme and omniscient power, an inheritance, that keeps the believer secure.

Even our faith in God is empowered by God. A Christian's continued faith is evidence of God's keeping power and protection.

"...who through faith are shielded by God's power until the coming of the salvation that is ready to be revealed in the last time." (1 Peter 1:5)

God Is Our Deliver

"For to be sure, he was crucified in weakness, yet he lives by God's power. Likewise, we are weak in him, yet by God's power we will live with him to serve you" (2 Corinthians 13:4). When the apostle Paul came to Corinth armed with the irresistible power of the risen, glorified Christ, he challenged folks to see that the God-Man, Jesus, was sent as a sacrifice for all who believe.

It is when we believe that we can trust. Jim Otto trusted God to help him through his circumstances and believed that whatever the outcome, his soul was safe in the loving arms of a great and mighty God.

God Wishes to Be Known

When it is all said and done, we can cherish those challenging ordeals because they will help build character, teach us our limitations, and allow us to share with others the saving grace of God. We can testify to others about the power of a living God. "Yet he saved them for his name's sake, to make his mighty power known" (Psalm 106:8).

This chapter is dedicated to the legacy of Pastor Bruce Miles, (who was called home to be with the Lord on November 19, 1999). He was a great friend and encourager to all who knew him. In the short time we knew one another, he provided me with wonderful insights into God's power and strength. These personal growth ideas come from notes on his desktop, left with his passing.

Personal Growth

- How does God give us the power to transform?

  Read 1 Corinthians 1:26-31

- How can God's power work within us?

  Read Ephesians 3:20

- How can we use His power to communicate to others His love?

  Read 1 Corinthians 2:1-5

- What is our strength today?

  Read Psalm 46:1

Chapter 9

An Elk That Changed a Man's Future

The Strength of God

In the summer of 1985 Larry D. Jones was managing 10 employees, writing estimates, and negotiating collision damage with insurance companies. His business, Acme Body and Fender Service, was his prime income source, so it was funding his passion for bowhunting and calling wildlife.

Larry had been hunting since he was eleven years old and realized he could call wildlife to himself by imitating animal sounds with his voice. A good friend, George Neil, realized most people didn't have the knack for voice calling, so he encouraged Larry to develop elk calls and instructional cassettes so others could enjoy calling elk. His reputation as an expert elk hunter and woodsman, and a superb elk caller, attracted the attention of Stony Wolf Productions, a Montana-based video production company.

Stony Wolf Productions wanted Larry to be one of the experts and editing consultants in an action-packed elk-hunting video. Two things clearly were obstacles to an all-out commitment by Larry: time to complete a successful hunt and his commitment to proclaiming Jesus Christ as Lord. He needed to sell the auto-body business so he would have time for the video project. Once the business was sold, he could direct his efforts and resources into developing and producing his game calls. Secondly, he needed the producer at Stony Wolf Productions to allow him to proclaim God's faithfulness.

The first obstacle evaporated when he sold his business in less than sixty days. But proclaiming his faith on video wouldn't be so easy—and even tested his faith and perseverance. It would be a time for Larry to measure his own heart and patience while leaning on God's strength.

Larry recalls, "I told them I would agree to do the video project as long as I could pray at the end of the tape, testifying to God's graciousness for providing the animal. With the help of one of the partners, Dale Burk, a Christian himself, an agreement was reached.

From the first day, Larry felt a unique challenge, a spiritual pressure of sorts, because he no longer was representing himself but the Lord. An impression came over him that this would be the ultimate test of his life. "Satan knew that if my testimony and confidence in God became publicly known, it might impact God's kingdom." Larry also knew that he needed a special kind of strength. It was the kind of strength that only God could provide.

Stony Wolf Productions' confidence in Larry's archery abilities, and a tight video budget, demanded they commit only a week to taping the hunt. Larry recalls, "I knew calling in an elk and bagging it in seven days was difficult, so having two guys following me with big heavy cameras would make our goal almost impossible." The pressure to succeed was challenging, and a cold front dumped six inches of snow on their hunt area, making the situation even worse.

Finally, on the fourth day, Larry called in a beautiful six-point bull to within twenty yards. As the bull moved within bow range, Larry crouched near a tree, nocked an arrow and prayed the bull would come to the call, so he would have a broadside shot opportunity. As scripted the bull emerged, stepped into an opening, and stopped broadside. It seemed Larry's prayers were answered. With great anticipation, Larry released. His arrow arched toward the lungs but smacked an unseen branch, which deflected it into the snow, just under the bull's chest. The bull leaped over a log and vanished into the lodgepole pine taking with him the chance for an over-the-shoulder-kill and Larry's closing prayer.

Three days later, the video team began packing its equipment, preparing for the trip home. After some discussion, it was decided Larry would continue to hunt and if he bagged a good bull, Stony Wolf Productions would send a cameraman to record the recovery.

The disappointment was almost too much to handle as Larry watched the crew members jump into their nice, warm car, even as he saw another front approaching. Larry was left in the woods alone to continue his challenge. After he had changed his location a couple of times, the elements became more threatening as Larry endeavored to find a good bull elk.

The cold continued, sometimes dipping below zero degrees. Larry hadn't anticipated the extreme cold. He wore all the clothing he had on hand and was still cold. Continuing to change locations, he managed to call in eight bulls, but none large enough or close enough to shoot. One four-by-five bull came within eight yards, but wheeled just as Larry was about to release.

It was the first time in Larry's life that he felt like giving up. He was lonely; he hadn't seen his wife, Miriam, in almost three weeks; he had lost nearly twenty pounds; the cold wasn't fun; many days he hiked fifteen miles in ankle-deep snow; and cold feet were the norm. Fatigue was setting in, and it was harder to keep mentally tough and to get out of bed.

One night, as he lay in his sleeping bag, he realized that his struggle was not against the weather, poor hunting conditions, or a trophy elk. His battle was with Satan over the right to encourage hunters to a godly life. To continue, he would need to seek God's power and encouragement.

During day twenty, Larry had hiked six miles, calling into every canyon. He finally had a bull answer and come to the call, but the bull circled. Larry tried to maneuver, but the crust on the snow popped with each step. It was impossible to circle in front of the bull. Later, after more hiking, Larry trudged up the trail, heading back to his truck. His exhausting ordeal was becoming more and more challenging because now the sides of his hiking boots had begun to rip apart from covering 200 miles of snow- and ice-covered terrain. "I remember asking God to give me the physical and mental strength to continue," he says.

Larry stopped to rest and decided to bugle from the trail. Suddenly, a bull's response cut through the silence, like a hot knife slicing through butter. Jones called again—he had not initially pinpointed the bull's position. Another screeching scream riffled through the timber. He was uphill from Larry's position. Larry quickly moved fifty yards toward the bull and moved into the shadows of a pine. He made some soft mews, and the bull growled and screeched back. "Please Lord, please make it happen" was his silent prayer as he again slipped forward. He slid in front of some bushy pines, nocked an arrow and made some soft cow mews.

Larry recalls: "The bull's rusty-gate-hinge scream was closer, and I instantly knew that the elk was coming. Remembering to record his bugles, I reached down to dig my tape recorder from my pack. I glanced up and saw the majestic elk striding toward my position. The stately-looking animal held its head high as its hot breath fogged the cold air."

Larry ducked behind a large pine tree and presented some of his best bugling calls. Like Al Hirt's playing before the New York Symphony, Larry played to the passions of this beast. "The bull became enraged and headed further down the hill, snorting and kicking up the new snow."

Larry became a little frustrated as the bull approached because it was circling right though clusters of pines. He didn't have a shot. "I needed the bull to walk to my left, so I cupped my hand and directed a soft mew to my left. It was incredible. Snow sprayed, and he skidded to a stop. He looked to my left, turned and walked until he presented himself broadside at fifteen yards. He stopped with his head hidden behind a tree."

Larry drew and released. The bull spun, lunged, and galloped downhill. His arrow had hit where intended, but the hunt had been the toughest and most frustrating he had ever experienced, so he cautiously followed the bull's crimson bloodtrail. One hundred yards later, Larry spotted the bull—collapsed and tangled in small trees.

"My eyes swelled with tears, and a lump in my throat caused me to gasp cold air. My whole body was shaking. I wiped my eyes while trying to hold back the overwhelming emotion. I walked forward, knelt, and gently touched the bull's side."

At that moment, almost in disbelief, Larry realized Satan had been defeated and God was going to be honored. "I prayed, giving thanks for the magnificent animal, God's creation, and for God's faithfulness, deliverance and strength."

Larry gutted the bull, and then walked three miles in the dark to his truck. He drove to a phone and at 1:00 A.M. contacted Stony Wolf Productions. They met him the next morning and videotaped the recovery—and Larry's prayer.

Larry thought his battle with Satan was over, but Satan never gives up. During the final video editing at the studio, there were more challenges to the strength of his convictions and character. One of the company's partners decided Larry's prayer at the end of the video should not be used. Larry reminded the partners of their agreement. Dale Burk and Larry stood strong in their agreement and convictions, and the partner felt the Spirit of God and consented to allow the testimony.

Dale Burk wrote the script for the scene, enhancing it. This experience became *Early Season Elk Hunting*, Larry's first elk-hunting video experience. Today, he produces calls, cassettes and videos. He now has more than twenty videos.

He Gives Strength to the Weary

Some people are wiped out by adversity. Others stand confidently in God's ability and character. They have an inner strength and immovable confidence that whatever the challenge, God will see them through it. Like Larry, they weather the storms (spiritual, emotional, and physical) that life brings. They press on with confidence and assurance as they stand fast in God's promises.

Our spiritual knapsacks are still not full. There is more we can learn about the nature and character of God. As hunters ready for the woods, we'll always want to have ready an assortment of equipment and strategies to be successful. So it is in life: The more we can equip ourselves with an understanding of God, the more effective we will be in life. Coping with trials and tribulations is all part of being alive. And for those of us who spend any time in the woods or on a desolate prairie, there is comfort in knowing that in addition to our skills, equipment, and preparations, there is a God who can provide the strength for our convictions so we can be victorious in our sufferings and trials.

Being victorious doesn't always mean we get our way or that God will provide a monster six-by-six elk. His ability to cope with our inabilities is His strength. Where we are weak, He is strong (see 2 Corinthians 12:9,10). Where we are incapable, He is able. When we are in a mess, He has a message.

King David reminds us of an important part of God's nature: "God is our refuge and strength, an ever-present help in trouble" (Psalm 46:1). God provides stability and strength for those who live in an unstable world. It is good to remember that our God is not a weakling. God has power and authority to help us out of any trouble, anytime and anywhere.

Temptation and trouble often drive people to confess God's power to save and protect. We see the strength and might of God through creation. Any observant woodsman can tell you about the strength of God as seen through His creation. The power of a thunderstorm, the awesomeness of a raging sea and the energy of a wild river all testify to His potency.

In light of God's strength, we are all weak. All that is really good and righteous is a product of a divine Creator—not of our own wisdom or strength. It is God who allows us to take each breath.

Like many of us, Larry D. Jones became weary of the challenge before him. But where many of us would have given up, he persevered and called to God for the physical and mental strength needed. He remembered the promise the prophet Isaiah and many other believers have seen fulfilled: "He gives strength to the weary and increases the power of the weak" (Isaiah 40:29).

Dealing with Loneliness

Like the apostle Paul, Larry had to deal with loneliness through an awareness of God's strength (see 2 Timothy 4:17). Paul was alone many times during his extended ministry. He was in an isolated jail cell when he wrote, "I can do everything through him who gives me strength" (Philippians 4:13). The Lord strengthened Paul to challenge those who would take his life without God's permission.

Paul went through shipwrecks, fatigue, famine, brutal attacks, and unfaithful friends, but he found that God infused him with strength as he focused upon his Savior and his own commitment to serve. He claimed the words that God provided to the prophet Isaiah:"Comfort, comfort my people, says your God" (Isaiah 40:1).

Paul and Larry both struggled with the same kind of loneliness. The quiet and persistent existence was a testimony to God's provision in their lives. The secret to their ability to cope with loneliness was their awareness that they had the privilege of fulfilling God's plan and purpose for their lives. It is this truth that has helped me through turbulent teenage years, through undeserved challenges to my integrity, through disloyal ministry partners, through three major surgeries (including a non-malignant brain tumor), and through the passing of three very close friends within a few months.

Even though I experience the strength and peace of God through every situation, I find that most ordeals really test my faith. If I don't seek out God's strength and comfort, challenges can push me toward my basic nature, causing me to forget the faithfulness and grace by which God has already helped me through previous trials. It is helpful to know that great saints, like the apostle Paul, also experienced recurring challenges to their faith.

Like many of us, Paul couldn't always change or fix his situation. But even in a damp, cold cell, he was aware that God was with him (see 2 Timothy 4:17). In Acts 18:9,10, Paul heard directly from God regarding the promised strength: "One night the Lord spoke to Paul in a vision:'Do not be afraid; keep on speaking, do not be silent. For I am with you, and no one is going to attack and harm you, because I have many people in this city.' "

What is it that you are struggling with today? Do you feel alone in your situation? Isn't it great to know that if you earnestly seek God, His strength can help you through difficult times?

Our sufferings and trials pale in comparison to what Christ experienced in the Garden of Gethsemane. It was a time when the sorrow and sin of all mankind were revealed to Him. He withstood the mental and ultimately physical suffering because He had God's strength coursing through His spirit. Jesus needed strength in His final hours, and God provided it: "An angel from heaven appeared to him and strengthened him" (Luke 22:43).

Steven S. Ivy, talking about the loneliness of Christ during that time, gives us an insight on how to use God's strength to deal with loneliness.

"Jesus frequently sought out 'lonely places' for prayer and meditation," he says. "Loneliness may be turned to solitude when it is dedicated to a cause, a project, or God. When loneliness turns to solitude, its promise is fully experienced."[1]

Reaching Out to Others in Strength

Like all of us, Gideon had his moments of doubt and his time of weaknesses. But he ended up being obedient to God and seeing that God's might and power are always better than ours. Gideon became a real role model and an encouragement to others as he worked through his greatest trial.

When the angel of the Lord came to him and said, "The Lord is with you, you mighty man of valor!" Gideon's response was, "O my lord, if the LORD is with us, why then has all this happened to us? And where are all His miracles?...The LORD has forsaken us" (Judges 6:12,13 NKJV).

Like our friend Larry D. Jones, Gideon was weary and frustrated and questioned his ability to accomplish the goal God placed before him.

The Lord responded in an encouraging way, "Go in this might of yours, and you shall save Israel from the hand of the Midianites. Have I not sent you?" (Judges 6:14 NKJV).

And Gideon went on to lead a small group of men to tear down the altar of Baal and, eventually, to destroy the Midianites. Here was the strength of God in harmony with the obedience of man. If you are obedient to God, you can expect His help with your challenges.

When God calls you to be strong, don't proclaim yourself weak. When through your obedience the Lord says you are righteous, don't see yourself any other way. If you declare yourself powerless, you negate the presence of God in every situation.

We come to the conclusion that our strength lies in the Lord and not in ourselves. Paul writes, "For the foolishness of God is wiser than man's wisdom, and the weakness of God is stronger than man's strength" (1 Corinthians 1:25).

There is no comparison between God and mankind when it comes to power and strength. He is infinite; we are finite. When we rely on the Lord, we have access to His unlimited power and strength. We will not end up a failure; instead, like Larry, we will accomplish our goal. The wise counsel of 1 Chronicles tells us, "Seek the Lord and His strength" (1 Chronicles 16:11 NKJV).

As we work through our trials, we will become role models for others.

The lessons Larry learned during his personal struggle to complete his project have translated into practical strategies that have been an encouragement to countless hunters. His character and integrity also grew during his lonely times with God. These lessons from his "wilderness experience" have helped others to connect with the strength of God.

Finally, the apostle Paul encourages us to use our experiences with God to help others: "Praise be to the God and Father of our Lord Jesus Christ, the Father of compassion and the God of all comfort, who comforts us in all our troubles, so that we can comfort those in any trouble with the comfort we ourselves have received from God" (2 Corinthians 1:3,4).

That is good counsel for a wise elk hunter and for each one of us who seeks to become more obedient to His call and more worthy of His strength.

Personal Application

- Have you ever struggled with loneliness? What does God's Word teach us about coping with our emotions during these challenging times?

  Read Acts 18:9,10

- How can you appropriate the strength of God for your life? What examples in Scripture help you understand His might and power?

  Read Psalms 28:7; 29:11; 46:1; 105:4

- What lessons from the wilderness have helped you to better appreciate the strength of God?

Chapter 10

Building Memories

The God of Comfort

As a father of twin sons, I appreciate the many wonderful family memories evolving from outdoor experiences that other fathers have shared with me. There is probably no greater gift you can give a child than your time. Someone once said, "Children need their father's presence more than his presents."

The great outdoors provides the backdrop for many wholesome memories to be captured in one's heart. As my friend Steve Chapman said, "While it's a fact that each time I go out I learn something new about a hunting tactic or a technical improvement to my equipment, there are greater lessons about life that I have 'bagged' that are now mounted on the wall of my heart."[1]

There is something about the tests and challenges you experience while seeking game that bonds father and child together in a special way. The fellowship between hunters is not ultimately based upon the equipment we share, where we hunt, or how many trophies hang in our dens. Our primary bond is that of personal sacrifice and shed blood. It is even more special when that companionship is shared with a family member, such as a son or daughter.

The personal effort required to match wits with a creature in its own environment often requires time, teamwork, and personal exertion that are unmatched in any other activity. Ultimately, there is the taking of an animal's life, which creates a sacred and honorable moment that is best understood by those we dearly love.

Each excursion provides opportunities for developing a deeper appreciation of our abilities as we rely on each other for strength, guidance and comfort. An abiding trust is developed between dads and their kids when life-and-death issues are at stake. The consequences for errors in judgment and inappropriate behavior are multiplied greatly in a wilderness setting.

My good friend and new hunting partner Brian Farley of Hayden Lake, Idaho, has a rich collection of great memories from hunting with his two sons. They have accompanied him on several major hunts all over North America. Brian loves to share his skills with others, especially with his sons. Through his guidance they have developed into very capable hunters.

Hunting is a way of life for Brian. His granddad and father infected him with the hunting virus when he was a young lad. It is a collection of lifelong memories of being in the woods that has given Brian a unique perspective on life and living. He has passed the same kinds of experiences on to his sons, knowing that time spent checking trails for signs, building tree stands and stalking a big buck with them would be precious and meaningful building blocks for their character and their appreciation for the Almighty.

Aw, Dad, Do I Have To!

Several years ago Brian sold his property on the Rathdrum, Idaho, prairie so he could buy a beautiful forty-acre spread on a Hayden, Idaho, mountaintop next to some of the best deer and elk hunting in our county. He built his family a wonderful house overlooking two meadow areas where game could be observed and their behavior recorded. It was being in this setting that led his youngest son, Travis, to challenge the hillsides with the same passion for hunting that marked Brian's life.

The late fall of 1997 found Brian sitting on his hillside watching two bucks fight over a beautiful doe. "I couldn't believe what I was seeing. It was as if I had a ringside seat to a professional fight," he says. Brian had been all over North America hunting a variety of animals and had seen some awesome sights, but none more memorable than what he saw that evening. "The bucks acted like they didn't care that I was even there. They chased each other around the ole burn pile several times while kicking up mud and weeds. They were so focused on their territorial dispute and the affections of that doe that they passed by me several times without even so much as a snort."

Brian returned home that evening to the dinner table as his wife, Pam, and elder son Chad, joined Travis in listening to a recap from Dad on all he had seen and learned from these three deer. He described the biggest buck as being a really nice four-point animal. Travis sat there and listened, then commented that sitting in the highest tree stand—called the "crow's nest" wasn't paying off; he had failed to see any bucks worth taking.

The next afternoon Brian and Travis headed out the door and began hiking to their spots. I have come to appreciate that Brian is a self-sacrificing guy who would rather see another person enjoy the success of taking a nice animal than keep the opportunity for himself. "Hey Travis, why don't you take the hill tonight?"

"Aw, Dad, I don't want to just sit there and stare at one spot. I really want to cover some territory and then climb up in the crow's nest for a better view of the area."

Brian remembered the impatience of his own youthful hunting experiences and could recall how hard it was to sit and look at one spot for any length of time. Brian tried one more time: "Son, I really want you to take this hillside stand and see if that four-point buck will use the crossing again. He's gone through two days in a row."

With some reluctance, Travis replied, "Aw, Dad, do I have to!"

Brian realized that comfort and encouragement are essential traits of a loving dad. He could see his son's disappointment in how the season had been going thus far and wanted to reassure him that all good things will come for those who patiently wait. One way Brian could soothe and comfort his disheartened son was to give him the best opportunity for success.

As a light snow began to fall, Brian directed his son to the open area on the hillside and walked toward the crow's nest on the other side of the property. About a half-hour later, Brian eased back into his tree stand chair when he heard Travis's rifle bark out. The shot pierced the silence with a deafening ring. Then he heard the familiar sound of the old .06 call out again.

Within minutes Brian hustled down the tree and made his way towards his son's position. Travis was standing over a beautiful four-point buck with a big grin on his face. "Dad, you were right. That deer came back across the meadow with his nose to the ground smelling for sign of his long-lost lover. I never did see the doe."

The two men celebrated and began dressing the animal out. Darkness quickly fell upon the hunters as they finished their chores. It was a perfect time for Travis to share with his dad how much it meant to be comforted and encouraged.

The Impact of a Tragedy

It was just a few short months later when Travis would be heading back home after pulling a double shift at work. He left work just after midnight and started the thirty-minutes drive home. Exhausted from the day's activities, he fell asleep at the wheel and crashed into a tree just a few miles from home.

It was about 4 A.M. when Pam awoke from a sound sleep and felt emptiness in the house. Brian and Chad were on a job out of town, and she hadn't heard Travis come home. She went to the front of the house and noticed that Travis' truck was not in the driveway. Then she returned to her bedroom window and looked out over the valley.

In the distance she could see the warning lights of several emergency vehicles illumining the prairie. She quickly dressed and drove down the hill to find her son's pickup wrapped around a tree.

Travis had not survived the crash. Within hours Brian and Chad had been alerted and returned to the gathering of bereaved friends and family at their home.

Shocked, Exhausted and Looking for Comfort

Finally the guests left, and Brian, Pam, and Chad were left with emptiness and pain that such an ordeal can bring. Brian recalls his grief: "There is no way to explain the feeling of loss, the depth of despair the complete bareness of spirit you feel when you lose a child. All I wanted to do was escape the constant pain I was feeling."

Lying in bed and staring up at the darkened ceiling, Pam and Brian searched their feelings and focused upon their loss. Minutes passed as they rested in silence fervently praying and seeking the comfort of God. Suddenly without any sort of warning Brian felt a force that seemed to virtually lift him off the bed. Not wanting to disturb Pam, he remained silent and just enjoyed the peace and warmth he was experiencing. "I'm a pretty logical and pragmatic guy. You have to be if you're a builder-developer. I rarely even think about extraordinary feelings. But this night was different. This was something that I had never experienced before."

After a few minutes Brian heard Pam shout, "He's here, He's here!"

Brian asked Pam, "Who is here?"

She said, "God is here! He just lifted me up in His arms...I felt His presence."

In the days, months, and years that have followed, Brian and Pam have continued to mourn the loss of their son—but they completely rely on and trust in God's continued comfort and presence in helping them through this tragedy.

Trials and Tribulations

William Penn once said, "No pain, no palm; no thorns, no throne; no gall, no glory; no cross, no crown."[2] The process of living life to the fullest has its moments of hurts, pain and suffering. For most of us, just the routine pressures of our stress-filled environment create demands that rip and tear at our character and spirit. For those of us with sensitive, caring natures, the critics and scoffers can pilfer moments of joy from our lives. Worry, fear, temptation, anger, and unresolved conflict are like thieves in the night that take every opportunity to steal away our delight.

The negative memories from the struggles and trials we face can rob us of joys and victories. Leon Bloy says, "Suffering passes, but the fact of having suffered never leaves us."[3]

Perhaps like Brian, who has hunted solo in some of the most remote back-country areas in the West, you may feel like many self-reliant woodsmen who consider themselves very tough without a need to be comforted. My friend, what trials are you facing? Are you standing alone? Do you feel supported and encouraged?

I've got really good news for you: We have a loving, caring heavenly Creator who really wants to comfort us. He stands ready to lift you up above your circumstances and help you through your enduring personal wilderness experiences.

When I want to know about comfort, I listen to people who have gone through a lot of suffering. Brian and Pam have endured. They join the apostle Paul, who was no stranger to major trials, pain, and personal conflict and who declared, "Praise be to the God and Father of our Lord Jesus Christ, the Father of compassion and the God of all comfort" (2 Corinthians 1:3). And like Paul, these two dear friends have come to really know the eternal mercy and comfort of God's love and peace.

God understands sorrow and suffering. In the New Testament alone there are nine different Greek words used to speak of sorrow, reflecting its commonness in man's life. Much like poison oak and poison ivy, suffering is woven through the forest of life. The story of the sufferings of mankind brought into this world through a rebellious spirit is a story of tears.

The death of a loved one represents the deepest, most heartfelt grief one can experience. The deep inner agony, which may or may not be expressed by outward weeping, wailing, or lament, is why we need a comforter.

Jesus was well acquainted with sorrow and grief (Isaiah 53:3). We are told of His weeping, His anger, His hunger, His thirst, and many other human emotions and characteristics. He knew the nature of man and the need for a comforter. In the Sermon on the Mount, Jesus underscores His concern for those who have grief and who are facing struggles: "Blessed are those who mourn, for they will be comforted" (Matthew 5:4).

Happiness comes to sad people like the Farleys because their godly sadness leads to God's comfort. "Come to Me, all who are weary and heavy-laden," Jesus says, "and I will give you rest" (Matthew 11:28 NASB).

I once heard the great preacher Charles Stanley say, "God allows tragedy to interrupt our lives so that He can comfort us. Once we have dealt with our hurt, He will bring someone across our path with whom we can identify and therefore comfort. This is part of God's strategy in maturing us. God is in the business of developing comforters. And the best comforter is one who has struggled with pain or sorrow of some sort and has emerged from that experience victorious. It is a very poor comforter who has never needed comforting." [4]

In His last days on earth, Jesus spoke to His disciples in much the same way a dying parent provides words to his children. In the thirteenth and fourteenth chapters of John's gospel we find words of comfort and encouragement that are reassuring to all followers of Christ.

In His words we find the heart of the Father and His love and comfort for His creation: I am going away; in My absence find comfort in one another's love (see John 13:31-35). I am going away; but it is to My Father's house, and in due season I will come back and take you to Me (see John 14:1-4). I am going away; but even when I am away I will be with you in the person of My alter ego, the Comforter (see John 14:15-21).

Jesus goes on to tell His disciples that if they believe in Him and the miracles He did, then they can believe also in the Father who sent Him. Jesus wants to encourage them to exercise faith in God, who will provide the Comforter for all their temporal anxieties. "Do not let your hearts be troubled. Trust in God; trust also in me" (John 14:1).

The Pure in Heart Shall Be Comforted

Jesus starts His discourse on the mountain overlooking the Sea of Galilee by telling the gathering, "Blessed are the pure in heart, for they shall see God" (Matthew 5:8). Being pure in heart means that we have asked God for forgiveness of sin. The Holy Spirit cannot comfort those who refuse to focus on God's grace. True mourning over sin does not focus on us, nor even on our sin, but on God Almighty. A repentant heart mourns over the sin that stands between itself and a perfect God.

Our sorrow and grief must be born from an obedient heart that has asked for God's forgiveness.

In his psalms David cried out, "For my iniquities are gone over my head; as a heavy burden they weigh too much for me" (Psalm 38:4 NASB), and "I know my transgressions, and my sin is always before me" (Psalm 51:3).

Dr. John MacArthur's New Testament Commentary on this subject is filled with insight and wisdom. "The result of godly mourning is comfort: they shall be comforted. That is why they are blessed," he writes. "It is not the mourning that blesses, but the comfort God gives to those who mourn in a godly way.

"As our mourning rises to the throne of God, His unsurpassed and matchless comfort descends from Him by Christ to us. Ours is the God of all comfort (2 Corinthians 1:3), who is always ready to meet our need, admonishing, sympathizing, encouraging, and strengthening. God is a God of comfort, Christ is a Christ of comfort, and the Holy Spirit is a Spirit of comfort. As believers we have the comfort of the entire Trinity!" [5]

God is the ultimate comforter. Comfort is not found in a bottle, or drugs, or an inappropriate relationship. It is not covered up with more work, power or prestige. And, as Brian has discovered, it is certainly not forgotten through escaping to the woods as we pursue our sport with an unbridled passion. No my friend, true comfort is experienced when we allow God's mercy to touch our hearts, to change our attitudes and to comfort our pain.

The apostle Paul helps me to summarize the importance of being a comforter: "If we are distressed, it is for your comfort and salvation; if we are comforted, it is for your comfort, which produces in you patient endurance of the same sufferings we suffer. And our hope for you is firm, because we know that just as you share in our sufferings, so also you share in our comfort" (2 Corinthians 1:6,7).

Open yourself to receiving the comfort of God as He encourages you to face your sorrow. The joys that God gives us through fond memories and joyful experiences help us endure the pain. The Farleys have a gallery of great memories and spiritual trophies of their beloved son Travis. What memories are you building that will help comfort you during those times of sorrow? Is the collection of animals in your den more important than the collection of memories on the wall of your heart?

Earlier I stated, "Our primary bond is that of personal sacrifice and shed blood" referring to the hunting experience. There is another more important experience where we share in the sacrifice of shed blood. As members of a family unite in their faith around the sacrifice and shed blood of Christ Jesus, we receive comfort in knowing that for all eternity we will be joined together in fellowship.

"Praise be to the God and Father of our Lord Jesus Christ, the Father of compassion and the God of all comfort" (2 Corinthians 1:3).

Personal Application:

- The tragedy that beset Brian and Pam challenged their faith. It also helped them experience more fully the comfort only God can provide. How would you handle this situation? What might be your response?

- In John 11:33-35 we see the compassion of Christ as He shows empathy for the grief of Mary and Martha related to the death of their beloved brother. According to John's account, "Jesus wept" (verse 35). What does that say to you about God's love, compassion and comfort for you during your struggles?

- 2 Corinthians 1:4 tells us that we will be comforted in our pain and suffering in order that we will be able to comfort others. Can you think of a situation you have experienced that could comfort someone else? Why not share it next time God places a person with a similar struggle in your life.

- What does 2 Corinthians 1:5 mean to you?

Chapter 11

The Ethics of Hunting

The God of Justice and Righteousness

I would be remiss to create a work such as this and not talk about the ethics and responsibilities associated with hunting. Hunting has always been one of man's deepest instincts and has fulfilled one of his greatest longings for significance. For the most part, hunting is an intimate activity requiring the utmost respect and appreciation for the wildlife being sought. Most hunters when pressed to the point will discuss their philosophy and ethics surrounding the pursuit of their passion; however, many will have little in-depth understanding of God's law of order for the outdoors.

Our forefathers hunted for subsistence; today's hunter is more focused on hunting as a recreational pursuit. For most people, hunting provides a renewal of body and spirit while providing delicious, low-cholesterol meat for the dinner table.

Any considerate hunter periodically has twinges of uneasiness when a beautiful, swift quail or waterfowl is brought down or when a graceful deer is arrowed. For a person who might find difficulty harvesting an animal or catching a fish, I suggest:"Don't hunt or fish!" If someone has a moral or ethical objection to taking an animal's life for human use, it is logical that he or she be a dedicated vegetarian and not require others in fish markets or slaughterhouses to harvest animals for their benefit.

Why hunt or fish? One of the most respected Americans of our generation is former President Jimmy Carter. Jimmy was raised on a farm and with his dad regularly participated in hunting and fishing. The former president, in a treatise on the ethics of hunting, talks about his reasons for participating in this sport: "My father and all my ancestors did it before me. It's been part of my life since childhood, and part of my identity, like being a Southerner or a Baptist."[1]

The former president and many other hunters I know share a similar understanding on the ethics of hunting. The companionship and challenges associated with this sport are unique.

There are many books and magazines on the subject that will educate and entice a person to pursue this activity. But although most hunters enjoy supplemental materials on the sport, reading cannot replace the personal experiences that are shared with more accomplished friends willing to teach what they know.

I have been made to feel more at peace about my hunting activities by my strict observance of conservation practices, my support of programs dedicated to increasing populations of wildlife, and my maturity as a hunter.

Stages of a Hunter

Ethical behavior in the woods is man's attempt at doing what is just, fair, and right. Temptations and our human frailties can present opportunities to compromise our integrity. When that big six-point bull jumps in front of our headlights an hour before hunting time, it is tempting to disregard the rules by taking an illegal shot.

I have found that ethical behavior is formed through a series of hunting experiences that challenge our commitment to be just and righteous. There is a certain maturity that develops as a seasoned woodsman evaluates what he has seen and heard from the mistakes others have made.

Robert A. Gruszecki in his book *The Wisdom of the Woods* suggests that there are five stages common to most hunters. Some hunters may reach the next stage and never go on. Some hunters may feel comfortable staying in a stage because they never realized the joys associated with the next level. Identifying these stages will also help the non-hunter to better understand why hunters do what they do. Reviewing the progression of maturity will help hunters to be more ethical and respectful of each opportunity.

The first stage is **the shooter stage.** This is a time when the novice hunter is becoming familiar with his capabilities and enjoying the preparations for the hunt. He is fascinated with his weapon and is learning to respect its power. Often a new hunter discharges a firearm numerous times at paper targets, cans, stumps, and the like, just to feel the control inherent in operating a gun.

The second stage is the **limited out stage** when the bag limit of the game is all-important. It is significant to this hunter to make sure others know of his success as he hunts. This hunter may or may not value the experience beyond the total bag limit for the hunt.

The next stage is the **trophy stage.** In this stage the hunter is very selective and may actually bypass an animal if it does not represent something of supremacy in the species. The experience tends to be measured in terms of "does it make the record book?" Some hunters never leave this stage; others combine it with the last two stages.

The fourth stage is the **technique stage.** The emphasis here is on the how rather than the what. Developing strategies, learning advanced stalking techniques, and utilizing more challenging equipment such as a bow and arrow, muzzleloader, pistol, or crossbow, the hunter explores methods for harvesting that require more patience and skill than simply using a rifle.

The final stage is the **master hunter stage.** This is a unique time in the development of a hunter when the emphasis is placed upon the experience itself. It is a period when the enjoyment is derived from the camaraderie of others, the peacefulness of nature, and the well-executed stalk, having game respond to your calls and the enjoyment of God's creation. In this stage a hunter may put down his weapon and take up a camera.[2]

At the end of the day, it is a hunter's obedience and concern for the unwritten rules of ethics, etiquette, and propriety that define the challenge.

It is a recognition that the effortless taking of game is not hunting but slaughter.

Perhaps Jimmy Carter summarizes my feelings on this subject best with these comments: "I have never been happier, more exhilarated, at peace, rested, inspired, and aware of the grandeur of the universe and the greatness of God than when I find myself in a natural setting not much changed from the way He made it. These feelings seem to be independent of the physical beauty of a place, for I have experienced them almost equally within a dense thicket of alders or on a high mountain in Alaska."[3]

A True Sportsman

Webster defines a sportsman as "one who abides by a code of fair play in games or in daily practice."[4] This certainly describes most hunters I know. Unlike many other sports that oftentimes find their sense of fair play governed by other competitors or spectators, hunting challenges an individual's integrity in a unique way. Despite the written regulations and a few dedicated game officers, for the most part the hunter must personally take on responsibility and control that test his honesty and integrity. Hunting is an intimate relationship among the hunter, the game and God Almighty.

A breach of trust before the ever-watchful eye of the Creator is going to be judged. Our ability to value His creation with respect and ethical behavior will affect our walk with God and our testimony to others.

In the grandeur of creation a hunter looks to his conscience and the watchful eyes of God to interpret points of law and common etiquette.

Early in the life of Ed Weatherby, his father, Roy, founder of Weatherby Firearms Co., instilled in the young hunter's mind the importance of being just and fair in his treatment of game. Ed valued the lessons he learned while in the field with his dad.

He remembers a time on his second dove-hunting trip he shot and downed an elusive dove. Ed recalls, "I was really excited about the shot. The dove came past my position when I squeezed off a round from my 20-gauge. As the dove was falling to the ground another gun went off. I wandered over to the area my dove had fallen only to find another guy picking up my bird. He told me he had shot it and that it wasn't my bird."

Ed's disappointment in the ethics and etiquette of that hunter became a vivid memory. The unfairness of the moment grabbed him and created a passion within his young mind to honor moral codes and principles of goodness.

Today Ed is a leader in the gun manufacturing industry as he encourages and supports conservation organizations. He has lobbied to enhance wildlife habitat while innovating safer, more efficient firearms for harvesting game.

Ed remains consistent in applying Christian principles to his personal life and his company's operation. "I believe in an ethical firearms company that promotes 'Single Shot Kills.' We do not make any semi-auto rifles or handguns. Assault guns or other firearms sought after by criminals are not part of our arsenal."

To look at a display of Weatherby firearms is to see quality and excellence in workmanship. The company has done a great deal to promote magnum ammunition that provides more accuracy and impact to allow for quicker kills. They have encouraged refinement in scopes, synthetic stocks, recoil brakes and folding rests. These developments have helped folks become more accurate shooters. All this testifies to Ed's desire to see a more ethical hunter who values the experience and privilege of participating in this sport.

A God Who Is Fair and Just

Ed Weatherby's approach to hunting and manufacturing is a good example of understanding the heart of God as it relates to fair and just treatment of others and wildlife. Because God is the absolute perfect model of justice, all human attempts at being fair and just seem powerless. Men like King David and the prophet Daniel acknowledged their own unrighteousness in contrast to the righteousness of God.

In the Old Testament the Hebrew word for "justice" also means "righteousness." Justice symbolizes the idea of moral fairness. God's judgment is the application of fairness to ethical and moral situations as related to a person's heart and intent.

Our God is perfectly holy and pure. His very Being cannot tolerate any type of sin or disobedience. Yet He is compassionate and merciful.

You may think that is impossible—and it is, for humans. But for God it is His character.

The attributes of God are never at cross-purposes with each other. A.W. Tozer puts it this way: "God's compassions flows out of His goodness, and goodness without justice is not goodness. God spares us because He is good, but He could not be good if He were not just.

"When God punishes the wicked…it is just because it is compatible with His goodness; so God does what becomes Him as supremely good God." [5]

When we deliberately break a fish-and-game law and are caught, justice must be served. There needs to be either a penalty or some sort of compensation for the crime.

In Charles Stanley's great work *Eternal Security*, he discusses some notes from *Ryrie's Bible Commentary* that will help us understand how a loving and merciful God can balance justice and mercy:

"If God is perfect, He is perfectly just. How can a perfectly just God make a guilty person (one who has sinned) not guilty? As Dr. Ryrie says in *Basic Theology*, 'There are only three options open to God as sinners stand in His courtroom. He must condemn them, compromise His own righteousness to receive them just the way they are, or He can change them into righteous people. If He can exercise the third option, then He can announce them righteous, which is justification.'" [6]

Dr. Ryrie presents a very important term: *justification*. To justify people is to declare them not guilty. According to the old saying, being justified is being "just-as-if-I-had-never-sinned."

Paul makes it clear that Christians have been justified (see Romans 5:1). To him, there is no conflict between God's justice and His willingness to justify sinners. He writes: "For the demonstration… of His righteousness at the present time, that He might be *just* and the *justifier* of the one who has faith in Jesus" (Romans 3:26 NASB, emphases added).

God does not camouflage the issue. He is not in the habit of pretending something is true when in fact it isn't. So how can He declare guilty men and women "not guilty"?

Paul sums up the answer to that question in his second letter to the Corinthians: "He made Him [Jesus] who knew no sin to be sin on our behalf, that we might become the righteousness of God in Him" (2 Corinthians 5:21 NASB).

God made a swap. God in some mystical way *charged* our sin to Christ and His righteousness to us. We were credited with righteousness despite our sinfulness, and Christ was credited with our guilt and sin despite His perfect life. Christ credited us with His righteousness, including all its rights and privileges. Wow! We are children of a King who owns the kingdom.

I have always been a little envious of guys who have private property or a good hunting lease somewhere. I no longer have to be jealous of their hunting privileges. As a child of God I'm an heir to all of His kingdom and universe.

Of course, I would not try to exploit this by trespassing on my neighbor's farm, as the local game warden may not hold the same view that I do!

When You Get Caught

The Old Testament book of Ezekiel gives us a very good example of how God's justice and mercy coexist. Through this prophet's experience we see how God judged a nation and, after the nation repented, restored the "true worship of the great Yahweh" with the development of the Temple.

About six centuries before the birth of Christ, as the Babylonians took over the holy lands, Ezekiel and 10,000 Jews lived in exile in the new Babylon empire. They lived as colonists more than captives, being permitted to farm tracts of land and own their own homes. The Babylonians taunted and shamed the Israelites because of their allegiance to Yahweh, whom they gleefully concluded was no equal to their own gods.

Israel willfully disobeyed God despite His kindness and blessings. They became self-indulgent while believing in idols and false prophets. God warned them of their sinful nature, but they did not repent. We can read in the eighteenth chapter of Ezekiel the challenges God gave the disobedient Israelites.

Israel became abusive and adulterous as their sexual sin became more sickening than what was seen in Sodom. The people of Israel would not acknowledge their guilt. They blamed their forefathers for their condition.

But God makes provisions for a just man. God remembers His covenant with Israel in her youth. He is gracious and always finds a covenant basis on which He can exercise His grace.

God gave Israel the inspired words of Ezekiel to guide their thinking. The prophet tried to direct Israel back to the concept of divine sovereignty, back to the obedience found in the ancient Mosaic covenants. By following this course, the children of God would repent and see God's righteousness. In a similar manner, the modern-day believer can experience how God's justice interacts with His mercy.

> *The words of the prophet ring true today as they did 2,500 years ago: But if a righteous man turns from his righteousness and commits sin and does the same detestable things the wicked man does, will he live? None of the righteous things he has done will be remembered. Because of the unfaithfulness he is guilty of and because of the sins he has committed, he will die (Ezekiel 18:24).*

The conclusion found in Ezekiel 18:30 suggests that a just God must judge each person for his own life. But He invites repentance, so that hope may replace ruin. The free gift of His Son's sacrifice will give us grace instead of the judgment.

> *The apostle Paul provides insight and assurance: "But because of your stubbornness and your unrepentant heart, you are storing up wrath against yourself for the day of God's wrath, when his righteous judgment will be revealed. God will give to each person according to what he has done. To those who by persistence in doing*

good seek glory, honor and immortality, he will give
eternal life. But for those who are self-seeking and who
reject the truth and follow evil, there will be wrath and
anger (Romans 2:5-8).

A Righteous Man

Like the Israelites of Ezekiel's day, we are all debtors to Him who is perfect. You say, "I'm not as vile and sinful as the folks pictured in this portion of Scripture or as bad as the people I see on some of the cop-type programs." But if we have broken even one commandment, we owe God a debt we cannot pay. Any sin and all sin is repulsive to a holy God. Because Christ paid the debt we cannot pay, we owe all the more love to God.

In the final analysis, we are all debtors to God's grace and His forgiving mercy. That is what makes Him totally righteous and fair. When Christ said, " It is finished" (see John 19:30), He meant whatever His people owed was wiped away forever from the book of remembrance.

How can we have our debts wiped away forever? We must believe and receive. We must acknowledge the God of the universe and thank Him for His lovingkindness by seeking His forgiveness and believing that Jesus died on the cross for our sins. After we ask for His forgiveness, we must receive Jesus as our Savior and Lord.

Ed Weatherby is successful and admired because he is a just and righteous man. His business practices and personal lifestyle suggest that he respects God's mercy and grace for the debts he accrued but was unable to pay. He knows that God's justice is what he deserves and is thankful for God's grace and righteousness.

Have you thought about the sacrifice that a loving God made for you? The only way you can escape His judgment is to receive His Son as your Savior and Lord. Do it today!

Personal Application

- What does it mean when we say our God is a just God?

  Read Romans 9:14-18

- What is the foundation of God's kingdom?

  Read Psalm 89:14

- How can you be a more ethical hunter and a more obedient follower?

- What do you think this statement means: "Through the work of Christ in atonement, justice is not violated but satisfied when God spares a sinner"?

  Read Leviticus 17:11

Chapter 12

The Ultimate Hunt

The God of Peace

Charlie Alsheimer is a name synonymous with whitetail deer research and hunting. Through the four books he has written, the two magazines he edits—*Deer and Deer Hunting* magazine and *Whitetail Business* magazine—and his 200-acre deer research facility, Charlie knows a great deal about whitetail deer.

Charlie's research and experience have helped thousands of hunters and photographers become more successful in their pursuit of this beautiful creature. The whitetail deer is one of the most respected and sought-after game animals in the United States. As an indication of its popularity, sportsmen who chase this critter spend more than fifteen billion dollars annually gearing up for the hunt and traveling to their destination. The phrase, "There's whitetails, then there's everything else when it comes to wildlife," is so true when talking about North American wildlife.

In the Old Testament we read about King David being a hunter. For this great king and Charlie "the ultimate hunt" in life is not the next trophy deer bagged but the hunt for God's heart. Charlie has learned that staying focused on God and at peace with himself is most important to being successful in deer hunting and in life.

Though he has encountered just about everything there is to experience in deer hunting, Charlie's real significance in life comes from who he is rather than what he does. Like many of us, Charlie learned this lesson the hard way. Having survived Vietnam and later the rigors of corporate life, he understands the trials and tribulations of the "real world."

In 1979, Charlie saw that the unhealthy pressures of a high-stress job were taking their toll on him and his family. He took a big leap of faith and decided to dedicate his life to helping others see God through outdoor communications. He desired to follow his passions and do something that brought joy and peace to his hectic life. Charlie recalls his feelings at the time: "There are too many people who really don't like their jobs and find it difficult to enjoy life. I was really tired of being one of those burnt-out corporate executives that missed out on the peace that God offers."

Charlie and his family quickly discovered that living off the monetary rewards of writing is the more challenging part of being an outdoor journalist.

Charlie knows that his decision to accept the Lord Jesus as his Savior in 1971 and his trust in asking Jesus to become Lord of his hunting affairs in 1979 were critical steps to becoming one of America's leading authorities on deer hunting.

Today Charlie knows a different type of pressure. It is the pressure to produce new photos, innovative articles, and annual trophy bucks. "Most folks don't realize the pressure placed on authors and photographers by editors and audiences to produce," he says.

"People will walk up and ask, 'What did you shoot this year?' They want to compare my success with other nationally known hunters. For some of the folks attending these gatherings, they want to first know that I'm a good hunter before they will listen to my testimony."

After his Vietnam experience and an emergency hospital visit in 1998, Charlie realized the important thing in life is to seek God's peace. He knows the challenges life brings can cause a person to focus on their circumstances rather than on positive solutions. "If we focus on our circumstances rather than on the peace that God provides, we can become suffocated with fear and concern," he says.

Let's Relax

For some time Charlie let the stress of being a successful photographer and hunter begin robbing him of the peace and joy he experienced in his work. Then he decided to listen to God's voice and receive the calmness of spirit that only our heavenly Father can provide.

Like many outdoorsmen, Charlie finds himself at peace with God when he is alone in the woods. An excerpt from his book *Whitetail—Behavior Through the Seasons* is an example of how he soaks up the tranquility of God's creation and spirit.

> *The early morning fog was as thick as honey as I stepped from the road into the dew-laden grass. In spite of near darkness I was able to negotiate my twelve-pound camera and tripod through the swale grass and tag alder. My goal was to make it to my photo blind along the edge of a shallow pond before the last white-tail bedded for the day. It didn't take me long to cover the three hundred yards and ready myself for the morning's offering. Dawn comes quickly in July and the rising sun began turning the sky's ribbons of clouds into a red and purple rainbow. With the light increasing by the minute I could see the thermals moving the fog's backlit beads of water back and forth. The sight was almost hypnotic. On the far side of*

the pond I could barely make out a muskrat swimming along the pond's shore. As I sat there gripping my camera I took in the blessing unfolding before me. The experience was so invigorating that I almost forgot why I was there.[1]

Only a man who is at peace with God and himself can fully experience the kaleidoscope of activity that occurs in nature. It is during those quiet, still times that creation unfolds its beauty and splendor to the watchful eye of the peaceful observer.

Experiencing Peace

We live in a hurried culture. Stress abounds everywhere as people seek after the American dream—success. Enough never seems to be enough. Gordon Dahl tells us, "Most middle-class Americans tend to worship their work, to work at their play, and to play at their worship. As a result, their meanings and values are distorted. Their relationships disintegrate faster than they can keep them in repair, and their life-styles resemble a cast of characters in search of a plot."[2]

For an outdoorsman lost in the woods or facing a life-threatening challenge, it is important to have the ability to find an inner peace that will transcend the circumstances and allow the person to find an appropriate solution. Most people reading this book will never face some of the grave incidents a few of us have encountered. Many folks find that the struggles and frustrations of everyday life are unsettling enough. In all our activities we need to find that special peace and comfort that only God can provide.

Almost everyone wants peace on earth. But nobody can guarantee permanent peace because nobody can control other people or circumstances. The peace of God is something we need to daily appropriate in our inner world even in the midst of the emotional storms that rage in the external world (see John 14:27).

It would be reasonable to ask, "How can we experience peace when family values are threatened by moral failures in government; incidents of outrageous violence plague our major cities; the threat of terrorism and disease permeates our culture; nature unleashes its fury through hurricanes, tornadoes, floods and earthquakes; and we have financial pressures that challenge our ability to provide for our family?"

Living life on this planet implies that we are all going to experience trouble in some form. For many it may even get worse before it gets better. The pursuit of materialism, power, prestige, fame, and fortune can cloud our lives with a dense fog that confuses our priorities. The consideration for those of us seeking a more peaceful life is not how we are going to escape times of trouble but how we can live with struggles and work our way through them.

When we have peace in our spirit, we feel a sense of quietness, tranquility, and stillness. There is the kind of calmness that Charlie speaks of in describing the summer morning around the pond. Did you know that God intends for us to live with that kind of peace? Why else would He have provided so many examples in nature and Scripture that beckon us to pursue a peaceful heart?

From Gideon (Judges 6), to King David (Psalm 29:11), to Jesus (John 14) and the apostle Paul (2 Corinthians 13:11), we are reminded that our God is a God of peace and comfort.

A logical question to ask is, "How do we experience peace in times of trouble?" Most hunters carefully prepare for their adventure by packing all the right survival stuff. In a similar manner, a prepared individual will make sure that the emotional tools necessary to cope with stress, pressure and anxiety will be part of his spiritual knapsack.

Over the past thirty years, I have had the privilege of listening to a number of great preachers who have shared numerous thoughts on this subject. There is no doubt that Pastor Charles Stanley of Atlanta, Georgia, has given me the most insight from God's Word on this subject. Like him, I hope to encourage those who want God's peace as part of their personal survival gear.

The apostle Paul tells us of the personal benefits we can obtain from having a peaceful heart: "May the God of hope fill you with all joy and peace as you trust in him, so that you may overflow with hope by the power of the Holy Spirit" (Romans 15:13).

Lessons on Peace from the Prince of Peace

If we want to know what the Father is like, we can look at the traits of the Son. The prophet Isaiah identifies Jesus Christ as the Prince of Peace (Isaiah 9:6). The peace we see in Christ is the peace of God.

The Prince of Peace has already won our peace to God by His death and resurrection. As believers we need not fret about finding God's peace because according to Paul we already have it. "Therefore, since we have been justified through faith, we have peace with God through our Lord Jesus Christ" (Romans 5:1). Our challenge is to appropriate it on a minute-by-minute basis.

The gospel of John contains a story that gives us some unique insights on how Jesus handled challenges, struggles and stress. Whether we are lost in the woods or lost in the fog of life, the principles that Christ teaches about God's peace can shape, if we let them, our future reactions and attitudes associated with comforting our inner spirit.

Our lesson on this principle is found the night before the arrest of Christ. Jesus had just finished providing a lesson on humility and service as He washed the disciples' feet. Trouble began to fill the hearts of the disciples as they heard Jesus testify that one in the group was going to betray Him; that another person would deny Him; that He was going to leave them and be crucified; and that the disciples would be persecuted for their loyalty. I believe that awful frustration and fear gripped their hearts. In the midst of their confusion and their uncertainty for the future, Jesus told them, "Do not let your hearts be troubled. Trust in God; trust also in me" (John 14:1).

Jesus wanted His disciples then and now to live with assurance, confidence, hope, love, and peace. As we continue reading John 14, we see that Christ went on to encourage the disciples by telling them about the hope of all believers in a heavenly place; that the Father is living in Him and that He speaks for God; that He promises a comforter, the Holy Spirit, who will be a counselor and guide; and that if people trust God they will have a perfect peace to endure their struggles. "Peace I leave with you; my peace I give to you. I do not give to you as the world gives. Do not let your hearts be troubled and do not be afraid" (John 14:27).

Everything the disciples depended upon was vanishing. They would experience the three darkest days the world has seen. Yet in a calm, quiet spirit, Jesus told them if they believed and trusted they could have a perfect peace. He was asking them to have a personal relationship to the God of peace by believing in Him, God's only begotten Son.

Jesus wanted them to know that the same God who is omnipresent, omniscient, omnipotent, eternal, and self-sufficient—the God who manifests His love and grace by being merciful, good, compassionate, kind, wise, and holy—the same God is capable of providing believers with the Comforter who can grant the peace to rise above their situation. He reminded them that only the Father could provide the quiet, calm, assured, pleasant, tranquil Spirit that will enable them to accomplish the awesome tasks set before them. The same God who equipped and protected the disciples can be our Shepherd, our Fortress, our Strength, and our Encourager who gives us the power to conquer our fears, anxieties and problems.

The Peace of the World

The wicked ways of the world influence us with temporal solutions to finding peace. We are encouraged to drink more, vacation at prestigious resorts, take more tranquilizers, change jobs, obtain more wealth, and find a new partner in life. Somehow these temporal objects will magically provide some sort of peace. Someone once said, "Happiness is not expensive, but families in America are spending millions trying to find it."

The peace the world offers tries to change the outward circumstances to create an inward peace. Ask any millionaire if their wealth, fame or position has really brought them peace. Any honest person will tell you that without the peace of God in your heart, the more you have the more unsettled life becomes.

The absence of peace in a life means that an individual will most likely be filled with anxiety, greed, anger, disobedience, addictions, and a poor self-image.

People get into addictions because they cannot satisfy the emptiness and loneliness in their hearts. For lack of real peace, they are tossed about in their wicked ways. " 'There is no peace,' says the LORD, 'for the wicked' " (Isaiah 48:22).

The logical question to ask is, "How can I get real and lasting peace in my life? Do I need to sit by a quiet pond all day long and look at the butterflies dancing through the air?"

Our sin separates us from God and His perfect peace. Until we accept Jesus Christ, the Prince of Peace, as our Savior and Lord, we cannot find true peace. Saul of Tarsus, who later became known as the apostle Paul, had no peace until he accepted Jesus as his personal Savior. "For he himself is our peace," exclaims Paul (Ephesians 2:14). Paul realized the importance of placing his heart and mind on the things of Christ, and he found perfect peace (see Isaiah 26:3). He could live in confidence and assurance because he believed in the power and comfort of a loving God. What about you? Can you claim that peace today?

God's voice brought about a deep calmness in Paul's spirit. He no longer was a man filled with rage and resentment; through his changed heart he became a compassionate companion to many.

Five Steps to Finding the Peace of God

What is it that causes us to be anxious? How does a person experience genuine tranquility? How can we know of God's comforting presence when our hurt is so deep, when our losses are so big?

Seek Out the God of Peace—Your Heavenly Father

1. **Focus.**

   When the world around you begins to fall apart, when you feel that you are lost in the fog of life, and when others are attacking you, remember His power and strength.

   God is our refuge and strength, our loving Father and provider. He is all-powerful and mighty, our keeper and stronghold, our helper and guide, and our Master and Lord. The sooner we focus upon Him as being our peace for life, the quicker we can experience a calmness and serenity that will give us purpose and passion.

2. **Trust God.**

   Set your trust in Him who is able. We should be assured and secure knowing that we are placing our confidence in that which is eternal. The Almighty, Holy God will never fail us or let us down. The answer to our concern may not always work out the way we think, but we can count on the peace of God being with us through the ordeal.

   "You will keep in perfect peace Him whose mind is steadfast, because he trusts in you. Trust in the LORD forever, for the LORD, the LORD, is the Rock eternal" (Isaiah 26:3,4).

3. **Study God's Word.**

   The Scriptures have withstood the test of time and the highest scrutiny. They are our anchor in times of personal storms. If we abide by His Word, we can find everlasting peace.

   God's Word cultivates godly attitudes, thoughts, and actions that will keep trials and temptations from overwhelming us. Right attitudes and thoughts must precede right practices. Only spiritual weapons will help in our warfare against the flesh (see 2 Corinthians 10:4). Pure behavior, in turn, produces spiritual peace and stability. We learn pure behavior from the Bible and not our ever changing cultural values.

   The prophet Isaiah writes, "The work of righteousness will be peace, and the service of righteousness, quietness and confidence forever" (Isaiah 32:17 NASB).

4. **Obey God.**

   The right attitude without the appropriate actions will not get us where we need to be. All our godly thinking is to lead to a practical end. Paul put it this way: "The things you have learned and received and heard and seen in me, practice these things; and the God of peace shall be with you" (Philippians 4:9 NASB).

Paul's words speak of action that's repetitious or continuous. When we say someone is practicing the violin or something else, we mean that person is working to improve a skill. When we say a doctor or lawyer has a practice, we are referring to his or her professional routine. Similarly, the word here refers to one's pattern of life or conduct.[3]

One of the wisest men to ever live, King Solomon, wrote these words to his son: "My son, do not forget my teaching, but keep my commands in your heart" (Proverbs 3:1).

5. Pray.

"Be anxious for nothing, but in everything by prayer and supplication with thanksgiving let your requests be made known to God. And the peace of God, which surpasses all comprehension, shall guard your hearts and minds in Christ Jesus" (Philippians 4:6,7 NASB). We are encouraged to thank God for His peace and His responses to our prayers. By avoiding anxiety through prayer and making other such attitude adjustments, we can "take captive every thought to make it obedient to Christ" (2 Corinthians 10:5).

The interesting thing about Philippians 4 is that God does not promise to give us what we ask for; He does not promise to meet our need immediately. What He promises is "the peace of God"—that is, the inner strength to endure until our desires and needs are fulfilled. It will surpass "all comprehension" because the unbelieving world will not understand our perfect peace.

Finally, "The God of peace shall be with you," writes Paul (Philippians 4:9 NASB), who ends on this note because he is addressing the issue of spiritual stability in the midst of trials. When we follow these guidelines, "the peace of God, which surpasses all comprehension, shall guard (our) hearts and...minds in Christ Jesus." There's no better protection from worry than that.[4]

"The ultimate hunt," and one of the easiest, is finding God and the peace only He can offer. Without peace in our hearts we will never be satisfied, even with a world-record whitetail.

Personal Application

- How can God help us during times of anxiety, despair, fear and anger?

- Review some of God's promises: Psalm 29:11; 37:37; 119:165; Proverbs 12:20; 14:30

- What do you want to change? What is troubling you today?

- How can you be still in the midst of a storm? Read Colossians 3:1

Chapter 13

Packing the Right Stuff

The Greatness of God

A good hunter is a prepared hunter. When you venture into the wilderness, you must be willing and comfortable to rely upon your survival skills, the equipment you carry, and your God-given instincts to overcome the possible challenges you will face.

While experiencing God's great creation can be alluring, it can present certain threats for the unprepared. In his book *The Wisdom of the Woods*, Robert Gruszecki discusses the spirit of today's hunter as related to participating in outdoor adventures.

> *There is a curious pressure to forests, valleys, mountains and meadows. The pressure is both physical and psychological. It drives us to journey out and experience the wisdom of the woods and the opportunity to get lost in the 'hunter's trance.' There are those of us who feel the pressure and answer the call to challenge the hinterland with a firearm, a fishing rod, or a bow. We must somehow conquer the hinterland...reduce it to a possession. This pressure has been a powerful influence on mankind since the dawn of time. It is an image that is at the core of our culture.[1]*

The magnetic pull of the outdoors was virtually irresistible and necessary for many of our forefathers. Subsistence-hunters found it a birthright for providing essential food, clothing, and shelter. The hunter was thought of as a hero in most cultures. He was looked up to as a person who was close to God's creation. The experiences he endured produced inspiration and insights that often encouraged others.

Today's hunter must be even more respectful of game management practices and have the courage of his convictions to help educate others on the value of the experience. As alluded to earlier, there is a sense of personal challenge and testing that helps shape and develop our character and spiritual sensitivity. Most folks who have gone through the tests and challenges associated with exploring the outdoors return to their communities as changed people. They become real assets because of their sensitivity, perceptions and appreciation for God and the expanse of His awesome creation.

Getting Ready

To maximize our experience in the outdoors, we must properly plan and prepare ourselves for the unexpected. Part of getting ready for the hunting season is getting in shape. I'm convinced that the motivating factor that keeps me on the treadmill and away from my wife's oatmeal cookies is the desire to hunt hard in a variety of terrains.

A good aerobics program not only makes sense from a health standpoint but also allows a person to participate more fully in hunting those more difficult areas. Many of the bigger animals escape to the far reaches where contact with man is limited. A lot of folks are roadside harvesters or quit at the first hill. A person truly committed to the challenge will move deep into the back country seeking his quarry.

I now live in the inland Northwest, where my hunting activities are year-round. From spring bear hunts to winter cougar and elk stalks, I must be ready and fit for the adventure. Being fit is no longer an option or seasonal thing. Every extra pound on my frame is additional weight that I carry up and down the hills I climb.

Also, I carefully select the equipment I pack so as not to be overburdened with gear that isn't necessary. Bringing along extra weight and bulky stuff can impede my efforts and consume precious energy. The following is a list of items most prepared hunters will carry.

Packing the Right Stuff

- Hunting license
- Rain gear, 45-gallon plastic yard bag or layered clothing
- Flashlight
- Survival kit containing signal devices, fishhooks, snare wire, energy bars, solar blanket, safety pins, lighter
- Water bottle with water purification tablets
- Map and compass or GPS unit
- First aid kit
- Sharp knife and sharpening rods
- Snake bite kit
- Sunblock
- Insect repellent
- Toilet paper
- Notepad and pencil
- Camera and extra film

- Rope

- Gloves and hat

- Whistle

- Balloon (extra water container)

Hunting Is a Marathon Experience

For most of us, hunting is like a marathon. It is a discipline of perseverance and patience. As easily accessible areas become more scarce and better public hunting spots become more pressured, we are going to be even more challenged physically as we fight our way into the remote reaches where game is more abundant.

Much like an athlete preparing for an event, the hunter will find himself mentally and physically challenged. When I think of the perseverance needed to be a successful hunter or athlete, I'm reminded of my good friend, All-Pro guard Steve Wisniewski, affectionately known as "the Wiz." In addition to his football duties, Steve loves the outdoors and has used his great size and stamina to his advantage in obtaining game.

Steve has received almost every honor available for his abilities on the gridiron. He has been asked to appear in eight Pro Bowl games and has been recognized by *Sports Illustrated* as one of the toughest guys in football because of his great strength and perseverance. Among his Oakland Raider teammates, Steve is known for his competitive spirit and dynamic power.

After playing his last game of the 1996 season, Steve sat in the locker room and reflected upon the difficult year the Raiders had experienced. There were numerous disappointments and lost opportunities that cost them a chance at a playoff game. He decided to commit himself to becoming an even better athlete and person.

Steve decided to prepare himself for a marathon run. The very next day, he met with his strength coach and asked for his help: "Coach, I really want to run a complete marathon. This is something I've got to do!"

The coaches were not excited about Steve's decision. They were worried that the tedious running could be harmful to his knees and back. They felt the constant pavement-pounding necessary to prepare for the long-distance event would ultimately take its toll on their valuable player's body. After all, linemen are not disciplined to long-distance running but to short and powerful bursts of energy.

His first effort at long distance was anything but glamorous. He ran a mile and a quarter and collapsed with his lungs burning. "I have never felt so challenged," he says. "My 308-pound body wasn't made to be tested in that way. I thought I was in good shape until I started jogging for distance."

The Wiz decided that preparing for a marathon was a good physical and mental discipline to prepare him for life. He had been a Christian since he was a young high school athlete but had never really challenged himself in his faith and personal commitment to serving God.

He made a decision. "Like the apostle Paul, I wanted to live a dedicated and committed life," he says. "I wanted to dedicate this marathon to God as a personal sacrifice and testimony of my consecrated life" (see Hebrews 12:1-29).

He remembered how the perseverance and dedication associated with hunting had helped shape his young life, and he knew that an even greater commitment would be required to further shape his relationship with God.

The marathon would serve as a metaphor for the depth of his commitment to serve the Lord. Steve fixed his gaze on the goal and began a disciplined daily workout that would ultimately lead to participating in the Olympia, Washington, Marathon on May 18, 1997.

Every day Steve hit the track with one thing in mind: "To honor and glorify God through this testing." Finally, after months of practice and losing thirty-eight pounds, he lined up with hundreds of other runners to begin the 26.2-mile journey to the finish line.

Physically, Steve knew he was in the best condition of his life. The real test would be the mental aspect of the run. He looked to God for the strength as he focused upon three verses:

- "Let us fix our eyes on Jesus, the author and perfecter of our faith, who for the joy set before him endured the cross, scorning its shame, and sat down at the right hand of the throne of God. Consider him who endured such opposition from sinful men, so that you will not grow weary and lose heart" (Hebrews 12:2,3).

- "Endure hardship as discipline; God is treating you as sons. For what son is not disciplined by his father? If you are not disciplined (and everyone undergoes discipline), then you are illegitimate children and not true sons" (Hebrews 12:7).

- "Do you not know that in a race all the runners run, but only one gets the prize? Run in such a way as to get the prize. Everyone who competes in the games goes into strict training. They do it to get a crown that will not last; but we do it to get a crown that will last forever. Therefore I do not run like a man running aimlessly; I do not fight like a man beating the air. No, I beat my body and make it my slave so that after I have preached to others, I myself will not be disqualified for the prize" (1 Corinthians 9:24-27).

Steve knew the odds of a man his size finishing a race of this distance were very slim. Though he had prepared himself well, the Wiz felt he needed some additional resources to get through the day. "I decided that I needed some music, food, and some pocket money. I bought a large elastic belt that held my Walkman, extra tapes, and some quick energy stuff. I hadn't practiced with this equipment and soon realized that the extra weight and bulk of everything really threw me off. It became an encumbrance to performing the way I had practiced."

After about four miles he realized the meaning of Hebrews 12:1—"Therefore, since we are surrounded by such a great cloud of witnesses, let us throw off everything that hinders and the sin that so easily entangles, and let us run with perseverance the race marked out for us." Steve ripped off the belt with all its weight and distractions and threw it into a nearby bush where he could retrieve it later.

It was five hours and thirty-three minutes from the sound of the starting gun when Steve crossed the finish line. He was the last person to finish, and one of very few folks over 270 pounds to ever finish a marathon. What he won was a deeper appreciation for the presence of God in his life. He realized the importance of working hard and persevering towards a goal. He recognized that the difference between ordinary and extraordinary is most often a little extra effort. Scripture encourages us to excel and work hard (see Ecclesiastes 9:10).

The Transcendence of God

In this book I have tried to identify some of the traits that make up God's character. We have discussed God's love, holiness, grace, mercy, sufficiency, omniscience, omnipresence, faithfulness, goodness, sovereignty, and comfort. The mightiest thought we can have is the thought of God. As with the Wiz, if our focus is upon God, we can receive and fully utilize the gifts He has given us. When we experience God in His fullness, we can really know His greatness and be more appreciative of the power and strength that are available to help us through our daily living.

Because God is a Spirit, the magnitude of distance, weight, and time have no meaning to Him. A marathon is but a yawn to a limitless God. His Spirit gives significance to all matter. While His very being transcends the universe and beyond, our thoughts and attention move toward those things we can more easily experience.

It is difficult for our finite minds to even begin considering the magnitude of the transcending power of God. There are those theologians who have considered this lofty thought and have left their impressions for us to ponder. While we appreciate their work, most folks feel intimated trying to comprehend their explanations. Many woodsmen may not be able to write eloquent thoughts about their impressions but can certainly testify to the spiritual feelings they experience while communing with God's creation.

In order to better appreciate those special occurrences, I encourage you to a greater understanding and appreciation of the magnificent vastness of the nature of our Creator.

There are no finite restrictions to God's divine presence, yet Jesus Christ His Son spoke of the Father being in heaven. Why? Christ was speaking about God's transcendence. He cannot be confined to a locality, such as your favorite place in the woods. The God whom we address is the God who is above and beyond the finite limits of the world. God is exalted far above the created universe yet concerned for every aspect of His creation.

"Indeed, the very hairs of your head are all numbered. Don't be afraid; you are worth more than many sparrows" (Luke 12:7).

God is able to transcend the expanses of the mysteries of the universe on the one hand and yet to have interaction with mankind on the other. God is so great that He cannot live on earth with man—but He still is most concerned for man's welfare. Except for Jesus Christ, King Solomon is described in Scripture as the wisest man to ever live. The son of King David discusses this unique paradox:

> But will God really dwell on earth with men? The heavens, even the highest heavens, cannot contain you. How much less this temple I have built! Yet give attention to your servant's prayer and his plea for mercy, O LORD my God. Hear the cry and the prayer that your servant is praying in your presence. May your eyes be open toward this temple day and night, this place of which you said you would put your Name there. May you hear the prayer your servant prays toward this place. Hear the supplications of your servant and of your people Israel when they pray toward this place. Hear from heaven, your dwelling place; and when you hear, forgive.
>
> —2 Chronicles 6:18-21

Who Is Above All Else?

There is a unique duality about God. He is above all else and stands apart from His creation, yet He is close enough to hear your whisper. We also have a duality of position when it comes to God. We are to know Him as intimately as we can, while in even our feeblest efforts we are to make Him known to others.

God is infinite in His creation; there is no beginning and no end.

"God is over all things," wrote Hildebert of Lavardin, "under all things; outside all; within but not enclosed; without but not excluded; above but not raised up; below but not depressed; wholly above, presiding; wholly beneath, sustaining; wholly within, filling." [2]

As you continue to fill your spiritual backpack with more truths about the character of God, it would be good to provide some extra room for the transcendence, or greatness, of God.

The prophet Isaiah, while comforting the Jewish exiles in Babylon, chose this message to help them grasp the vastness and magnitude of His being:

> Who has measured the waters in the hollow of his hand, or with the breadth of his hand marked off the heavens?
> Who has held the dust of the earth in a basket, or weighed the mountains on the scales and the hills in a balance?
> Who has understood the mind of
> the LORD, or instructed him as his counselor?
> Whom did the LORD consult to enlighten him,
> and who taught him the right way?
> Who was it that taught him knowledge
> or showed him the path of understanding?
> Surely the nations are like a drop in a bucket;
> they are regarded as dust on the scales;
> he weighs the islands as though they were fine dust.
> Lebanon is not sufficient for altar fires,
> nor its animals enough for burnt offerings.
> Before him all the nations are as nothing;
> they are regarded by him as worthless
> and less than nothing.
> To whom, then, will you compare God?
> What image will you compare him to?
> As for an idol, a craftsman casts it,
> and a goldsmith overlays it with gold
> and fashions silver chains for it.
> A man too poor to present such an offering
> selects wood that will not rot.
> He looks for a skilled craftsman
> to set up an idol that will not topple.

Do you not know?
Have you not heard?
Has it not been told you from the beginning?
Have you not understood since the earth was founded?
He sits enthroned above the circle of the earth,
and its people are like grasshoppers.
He stretches out the heavens like a canopy,
and spreads them out like a tent to live in.
He brings princes to naught
and reduces the rulers of this world to nothing.
No sooner are they planted,
no sooner are they sown,
no sooner do they take root in the ground,
than he blows on them and they wither,
and a whirlwind sweeps them away like chaff.
"To whom will you compare me?
Or who is my equal?" says the Holy One.
Lift your eyes and look to the heavens:
Who created all these?
He who brings out the starry host one by one,
and calls them each by name.
Because of his great power and mighty strength,
not one of them is missing.
Why do you say, O Jacob,
and complain, O Israel,
"My way is hidden from the LORD;
my cause is disregarded by my God"?
Do you not know?
Have you not heard?
The LORD is the everlasting God,
the Creator of the ends of the earth.
He will not grow tired or weary,
and his understanding no one can fathom.
He gives strength to the weary
and increases the power of the weak.

Even youths grow tired and weary,
and young men stumble and fall;
but those who hope in the LORD
will renew their strength.
They will soar on wings like eagles;
they will run and not grow weary,
they will walk and not be faint.

—Isaiah 40:12-31

Eliminating the Encumbrances

A good hunter will carry only those things that are essential to his survival. All other items may be seen as excessive or burdensome. If we think of life as being like a marathon race, we can appreciate the lessons learned from carrying too much weight in our packs. Like Steve, if we are to run a good race, we need to properly prepare by throwing off those encumbrances that weight us down.

If God is everywhere at all times, then we cannot escape His presence or His knowledge of our "extra baggage." As the Psalmist put it, "Where can I go from your Spirit? Where can I flee from your presence?" (Psalm 139:7).

The most encumbering baggage in our lives can be sin.

There is no one who has not sinned (see 1 Kings 8:46; Romans 3:23). To some degree we are all carrying extra baggage (sin) that encumbers our progress. You may ask, "What is this encumbrance we call sin?" Sin is that which is in opposition to God's benevolent purposes for His creation. According to the Bible writers, sin is an ever-present reality that enslaves the human race and has corrupted God's plan for His creation. The concept of sin is, first and foremost, a religious concept, because all sin is ultimately against God—God's laws, God's creation, God's covenant, and God's purposes. It is the basic corrupting agent in the entire universe.

There are numerous Hebrew and Greek words used to designate sin in the biblical writings. Perhaps the most basic is the idea that when we sin it is a "revolt" or a "transgression" and indicates a deliberate act of defiance against God. This idea lies at the heart of the Genesis account of the beginning of sin (Genesis 3:1-7), where the essential problem lies in the desire of the humans to "be like God." All sin is an act of idolatry—the attempt to replace the Creator with someone or something else, usually one's own self or one's own creation. Paul understood this very well, as he indicates in Romans 1:18–3:20. All humankind lies under condemnation because all are idolaters of one type or another.

Stay Fit and Pack Lighter

We become more successful hunters if we are able to keep our focus, persevere in our fitness and pack fewer things that might encumber our progress. So it is in the quest to grow more intimate with our Creator. We need to focus on the truth of His presence, being persistent in building good character and eliminating the sin that encumbers us. We do this by staying spiritually fit.

Next time you're in the woods or on that prairie, stop and think about how you could better relate to the God who created all that you love. He is patiently waiting for you to explore a deeper relationship with Him. The greatest hunt of all is the reward you will receive when you capture the essence of His greatness and character. Good hunting!

Personal Application

- Would you like to better know the character of God? To really know and love Him is to know and love Jesus, His Son.

  Read John 10:30; John 14; Matthew 28

- What do you see in God's creation that helps you understand the vastness and greatness of His work?

- When do you feel closest to God and why? Are you willing to explore other areas or relationships that might expand your understanding of His character?

- How are you comforted by these words, spoken by Jesus: "and lo, I am with you always, even to the end of the age"? (Matthew 28:20 NASB).

Chapter 14

A View from a Tree Stand

God Is Ever Present

How many times have you wished there were some sort of sky hook to lift you high above the brushy forest so that you could gain a better perspective of the area? Finding game is never easy and can be particularly difficult in dense vegetation.

I'm basically a spot-and-stalk type of hunter who likes to carefully explore the surrounding terrain looking for sign and trails where a deer might return. I cover a lot of ground when hunting, but still don't have the ultimate perspective on the territory.

Being a good hunter means using all knowledge, equipment and techniques to refine your skills and abilities. In part, I hope this book is a testament for those wishing to learn about hunting or for those wanting to expand their knowledge of this unique sport. This chapter offers the hunter a glimpse into an evolving technique that is becoming a major factor in helping many hunters become more consistent in their harvest.

Oftentimes spot-and-stalk hunters will scare off the animals before they even have a chance to see their quarry. Despite using a great deal of care, a stalker's scent, movement

171

or noise will alert the critters of impending danger. All this can work to the disadvantage of even a good hunter. Ground hunting limits us in space and proximity.

Our view and approach to a given area are defined by the terrain, wind direction, and weather patterns we encounter. While I really like to ground hunt with my Mathews compound bow, I sometimes find it difficult to move about really brushy terrain with all the archery gear I need to carry. Fortunately, there is a solution to my problem.

Tree-Stand Hunting

Tree-stand hunting has grown in popularity during the past decade. As more folks become involved with archery hunting, a less active hunter can now place himself in a position where he can harvest an animal without a lot of physical exertion. The hunter can now focus his concentration on shot placement, rather than worrying about wind direction, noise, and scent problems.

Recently I was speaking with a good friend, hunter, author and musician, Steve Chapman. He lives in Tennessee, where there is excellent whitetail deer hunting. He reminded me of all the benefits associated with a good tree stand. In surveying the various hunting catalogs, I noticed a significant increase in the number of companies producing stands. There are ladder stands, Loc-On-Limb stands, climbing stands, trunk stands and permanent frame stands that all perform in a similar way. Our mutual friend Paul Meeks of API Treestands, has perfected many of the tree-stand strategies that have helped hunters like Steve and me become more effective with this method of hunting.

The nature of a stand is to get the hunter above ground level so that he might have a greater view and presence over the area to be hunted. As you increase the elevation, you expand the acreage you view. This helps you detect animals moving about in a selected area. You can see the deer quicker, allowing you to take longer to make decisions relative to harvesting that particular animal.

Seeing without being seen is the essence of stealth. Being above the normal sight line and having your scent off the ground allows you to escape the casual scan of a wary animal. Typically animals scan the horizon for danger and do not look up. Most predators that could threaten the deer live on the ground, where they are quickly detected by an alert deer.

Tree-stand hunts also allow the hunter to bring along extra supplies, clothing and equipment that might be too bulky or cumbersome for the ground hunter. Life in a tree stand can be pretty comfortable.

Tree stands are particularly effective for hunting selected game in areas where there is some degree of predictability. Whitetail deer tend to develop predictable patterns that provide a hunter with information that will help him select an area and time when the animal might return. A favorite rub area or watering hole may be visited at selected times during the day. Though stands can be used to hunt almost any species, the comments in this chapter are specifically for deer hunters.

I have discovered that in areas where there is significant brush, without many open pasture areas, animals tend to be more random in their meanderings, making it difficult for the hunter to predict behavioral patterns. Tree stands in this type of country have limited benefits. But in areas where there exist scattered meadows, marshes, and farmlands with limited heavy cover, animals can be a little more predictable in their wanderings.

A tree-stand hunter needs to spend considerable time scouting an area before locating his stand. Typically a stand should be placed where there is a great deal of animal activity. Rub areas, bedding spots, well-used trails and areas with nearby, good food sources all provide suitable tree-stand sites.

The more you can "think like a deer," the better the odds will be that you will place your stand in the best location.

It is good to have three or four tree-stand locations in a given area. If one area doesn't seem to be active, you can easily move to another stand. It is best to place your stand in the tree several days ahead of time. If animals detect the stand, they can adjust to the intrusion without changing their patterns. Most stands are portable and can be easily moved to a new area in the middle of the day if the first location doesn't pay off. It is important to remember that you don't journey to your stand on the same path that the animals are using. Your scent may be noticed and could alert the deer to your presence.

What constitutes a productive area for a tree stand? Remember, deer are primarily driven by three basic needs—food, water and reproduction. They seek protected areas where they can freely romp and roam. Abundant food and water supplies with good bedding places will exist in prime locations. The following is a list that will help you find the most probable areas to place a stand.

- **Food Source**—Choose an area where there is an abundance of grasses, bushes, nuts, fruits, or mushrooms. Late in the season, the deer tend to concentrate on areas that have a good supply of foods high in protein. Places with oak trees or fruit trees are especially good areas to scout.

- **Scrape Areas**—Bucks like to rub their antlers on saplings to mark their territory. And as the antlers begin to harden, they rub the velvet off the antlers using small trees and brush. Look for trees that have bark worn off and feel wet to the touch. This would be a fresh scrape.

- **Trail Activity**—Deer usually find the path of least resistance. They will follow gently sloping contours with the greatest cover offering good protection. Look for well-worn trails with a lot of hoof marks and deer droppings.

- **Water Crossing**—Deer prefer to cross creeks or rivers at a point where the water is the lowest. Check the banks out for more hoof prints.

- **Funnel Areas**—Deer will move along wooded perimeters next to open fields. At the point where the fields connect, there is a funnel effect as game are channeled into concentrated areas.

- **Watering Holes**—Like any other creature, deer require water—and lots of it. Any well-worn watering hole is a good place to setup a stand.

- **Wind Direction**—Always try to place your stand downwind from the attracting area. If the prevailing wind is from the northwest as it crosses the well-worn trail, then place your stand in a tree on the southeast side of the trail.

The Scent of Man

Earlier we mentioned the concern for human scent in an area that deer frequent. Any good deer or elk hunter can tell you that your scent will permeate the woods. Deer will often smell you long before they see you. Despite being careful about washing with scentless soaps and properly storing your clothing, you emit odors that can give away your presence.

Don Wyatt, president of Snake River Scents of Spirit Lake, Washington, is an expert on researching and developing scents that either attract animals or coverup unnatural odors. His Stick-O-Scent is like a deodorant stick and can be rolled onto anything.

Don tells us, "A good stick scent combined with some game calls will increase the opportunity to bring in an elk or deer by at least seventy-five percent. We now have various scents that take into account the seasonal cycles of the animals. A good scent is specifically designed to attract game during the summer, pre-rut, rut and post-rut cycles."

Steve Chapman and I believe many animals, especially deer and elk, have olfactory glands that have an acute ability to distinguish scents. Molecules of sweat, body odor or even bad breath will alert the animal to your presence. Deer and elk have developed sensitivities to the presence of man that will affect their behavior.

The Hazards and Benefits of Tree Stands

While tree stands provide a better perspective of the area, they have some inherit hazards that need to be evaluated. "An accurate statement is probably that the only people who don't fall out of tree stands are the ones who don't use them," states master hunter John Phillips.[1]

By their nature, some tree-stand hunters tend to take risks that are unwarranted. They climb trees that are rotten and dangerous. Often old wooden platforms have rusted nails or rotten timber, making them a real hazard for the unsuspecting hunter. Once in a comfortable stand, some hunters get so relaxed that they sometimes fall asleep and out of their stands. An essential piece of equipment for every stand hunter is a safety belt. Anyone hunting from a tree stand should be very safety-conscious by anticipating the hazards that being suspended with a weapon in a tree might bring.

I personally don't like heights, and I see additional risk if I get above fifteen feet high in a stand. I also like to stand up in a stand, thereby keeping more alert and in a better position to draw back my bow. After thirty to forty-five minutes of standing, I will sit for ten minutes, then return to my standing position. Railings and safety belts help me feel secure in my movements.

Good camouflage clothing and a background of tree limbs and leaf cover help eliminate your silhouette from the sky-line. Placing a stick scent upwind from your blind also offers some attracting elements to the scene.

When in the tree stand, keep your eyes constantly moving, looking for anything out of the ordinary. Remember to periodically check the area behind you. Steve Chapman recalls a time when he was hunting during the muzzle-loading season and had placed his stand near a "hot scrape-line" along an old logging road.

Steve recalls, "It was a perfect early winter day. The air was fresh and clean with a slight breeze coming towards my stand. I placed some scent around the area to help draw the deer to my position. I had been in my stand about thirty-five minutes thinking about the great vantage point this gives me on the whole scene. I had the ability to somewhat predict what was going to happen before it happened. I had a perspective on the woods that could only be obtained from a high vantage point."

Having a good perspective on hunting and life is a key to Steve's success in every area.

"I remember looking over my left shoulder when I saw this beautiful nine-point buck," Steve says. "He was a beauty. He carefully looked all around, keeping his nose close to the ground, trying to pick up on anything that might alert him to danger. He was the biggest deer I had seen in quite some time."

Tennessee has an abundance of whitetail deer. A hunter can take multiple animals in a year, so Steve gets plenty of practice with a variety of hunting equipment.

Chapman recalls, "The animal continued to move to my left, putting me at a real disadvantage in that I'm right-handed. The woods were especially quiet that morning, so I needed to be extra careful moving about in my stand as every little sound was going to be heard by this wary animal."

A difficult shot for any hunter is a shot taken from the back side of the stand. He must be very careful about falling out of the stand or giving away his position with excessive movement or noise as he leans and twists around the tree for the shot.

Steve was mindful of this concern and carefully eased his muzzleloader to his left shoulder. "It meant I had to shoot with my left-hand position. Carefully aiming with my left eye, I closed my dominant right. Fortunately I was able to squeeze off the shot when the buck was within twenty yards of my position. He dropped like a lead balloon. I lowered my gun down and reloaded before I moved toward the big buck. I gave thanks to God for the opportunity to take such a fine animal. What a day!"

Perspectives from a Tree Stand

Tree stands have their limitations. For a given period of time, you are committed to survey one area. Even with an elevated view of the terrain, you still can't be in all places at the same time. If you place your stand at the old watering hole, that morning the deer will probably show up at the scrape area.

As Steve and other tree-stand hunters have experienced, a stand gives you a unique perspective on the area you are hunting. And so it is with God. He has a unique perspective on mankind. He has been hunting for man's heart from the beginning of time. Unlike the limitations we face, God is ever present in the universe. We call this trait omnipresence.

The *Nelson New Illustrated Bible Dictionary* contains this entry:

> OMNIPRESENCE [om nih PRES ence] — a theological term that refers to the unlimited nature of

God or His ability to be everywhere at all times. God is not like the manufactured idols of ancient cultures that were limited to one altar or temple area. God reveals Himself in the Bible as the Lord who is everywhere. God was present as Lord in all creation (Psalm 139:7-12), and there is no escaping Him. He is present in our innermost thoughts. Even as we are formed in the womb, He knows all the days of our future (Psalm 139).

God sees in secret and rewards in secret, as Jesus taught His disciples; He looks not only on outward actions, but especially on the inner attitudes of a person's heart (Matthew 6:1-18). Because God is the Creator and Sustainer of time and space, He is everywhere. Being everywhere, He is our great Comforter, Friend, and Redeemer.[2]

Added to our spiritual backpack, this trip is our understanding of the infinite existence of a supreme Being. God is not limited by space, and is present in every point of space with His whole being. The prophets who wrote 1 Kings had a good understanding of this concept when they penned these words: "But will God really dwell on earth? The heavens, even the highest heaven, cannot contain you. How much less this temple I have built!" (1 Kings 8:27).

The Scent of God

Many hunters I've talked to say, "I feel close to God when I'm out hunting." They tell of a certain aura or feeling they have about the presence of God in their lives. I'm convinced it is not the place so much as the state of mind. If we stop long enough to listen and feel God, then we can experience Him. God is everywhere at the same time. His being fills everything (see Jeremiah 23:24; 1 Kings 8:27).

The importance of feeling God's presence cannot be overemphasized. The idea that God is at once far off and near at the same time is difficult for the human mind to comprehend. Scripture tells us that God is infinite. This means that His being knows no limits. There can be no limit to His presence. "God is over all things," wrote Hildebert of Lavardin, "under all things; outside all; within but not enclosed; without but not excluded; above but not raised up; below but not depressed; wholly above, presiding; wholly beneath, sustaining; wholly within, filling."

For the Christian there is a deep sense of comfort and realism to the "practice of the presence of God." This isn't about some weird mind game but about a real relationship with the great Jehovah. It is the recognition that there is a real presence of the One whom the prophets of old, Jesus Christ, and all sound biblical teaching point to as already being present.

Among the many lessons I have learned about the character of God is the importance of adopting the challenge found in Psalm 46:10: "Be still [cease striving] and know that I am God." To some degree, our modern "seeker-targeted" churches have placed such a premium on church growth and reaching the lost that we have lost our religious awe and our consciousness of the presence of the Almighty.

It feels like we have misplaced our spirit of worship and our ability to withdraw inwardly to meet God in adoring silence. Our sense of majesty has been replaced with slick marketing programs that tend to place our attention on numbers rather than on experience.

I have rediscovered the importance of feeling God's presence. Life depends upon it, for God gave us life. When we drift away from Him, life becomes dark and all manner of unhappiness plagues us. When we return to Him, life is renewed and becomes fresh, sparkling, delicious.

Knowing God Is With You

Many times a hunter will experience the unique sensation that "I'm not the only one in the woods." You will sense that there are critters watching over you. You may not see or hear them, but you can intuitively feel their presence.

In a similar manner, a believer can know that God is with him. He feels God's presence. Once you have asked God into your life, you will experience His grace and love as they illuminate your life.

There is not enough room in this chapter to describe all the ways we know God is with us. Let's quickly look at four affirmations of how God's presence helps keep us on track with His will for our lives.

- **Forgiveness of sin**—We can't escape God and His ultimate judgment. The Psalmist declares, "Where can I go from your Spirit? Where can I flee from your presence?" (Psalm 139:7).

When a person comes before the Almighty and seeks forgiveness for his sins, he will experience a special peace and consolation that only God can provide. The apostle John shares his ideas on this matter as interpreted in the Living Bible: "This is the message God has given us to pass on to you: that God is Light and in him is no darkness at all. So if we say we are his friends but go on living in spiritual darkness and sin, we are lying. But if we are living in the light of *God's presence*, just as Christ did, then we have wonderful fellowship and joy with each other, and the blood of Jesus his Son cleanses us from every sin" (1 John 1:5-7 TLB, emphasis added).

- **Comfort during weakness**—The apostle Paul testified to the comfort he felt during times of weakness. The weaker he was, the more he was energized by God's presence and power and, therefore, the stronger he was. There is no pleasure that can be taken from infirmities, reproaches, requests, persecutions, or distresses unless this is the case. But if we believe that God's grace and mercy are manifested even more in our lives, the deeper our pain or the greater our adversity, the more we can experience His presence.

He is always there as our comfort: "Let your gentleness be evident to all. The Lord is near. Do not be anxious about anything, but in everything, by prayer and petition, with thanksgiving, present your requests to God" (Philippians 4:5,6).

The apostle Paul also tells us, "For in Him we live and move and have our being" (Acts 17:28). Our vitality, our energy, and even our being depend upon knowing and experiencing God and the fullness of His character. You can sense His presence and be renewed if you take the time to really know Him.

- **It removes loneliness**—Even if we are rejected and abandoned by family, friends, or even fellow believers, we know that our heavenly Father will never leave us (Hebrews 13:5). King David experienced considerable loneliness when Saul, a father figure, rejected him. He was a fugitive in the wilderness except for God's presence. He cried out to God:

> Though my father and mother forsake me,
> the LORD will receive me.
> Teach me your way, O LORD;
> lead me in a straight path
> because of my oppressors.
> Do not turn me over to the desire of my foes,
> for false witnesses rise up against me,
> breathing out violence.
> I am still confident of this:

> I will see the goodness of the LORD
> in the land of the living.
> Wait for the LORD;
> be strong and take heart
> and wait for the LORD.
> —Psalm 27:10-14

To drive away loneliness, God's presence is all a believer ever needs.

My friend, living the Christian life is acting as if everything is in the presence of God—because it is. Take some time to really know Him. If you are a follower, He is present in your life today. Seek His loving face and He will comfort and guide you.

Whether you are a tree-stand hunter, a ground hunter, or just someone who enjoys being in God's great outdoors, seek the presence of God in life. His presence isn't just available in outdoor settings. God is with you in an emergency room of a hospital, in a stressed work environment, in the middle of a family argument, and in the quietness of your personal prayer time. God is ever present and always available. Unlike our favorite sports store, He is open for business twenty-four hours a day.

He can give us that proper perspective, the big overview that only the God of all creation has. He is our "eternal eye in the sky" that can see and prepare us for the events of tomorrow while helping us work through the struggles of yesterday.

You never have to worry about falling out of God's tree stand. He is our safety belt and the One who comforts us in our falls.

Personal Application

* In Old Testament times the word "face" often meant "presence.""The face of God," His gracious presence, is an important truth to capture. When was the last time you experienced the face of God? How can you duplicate that experience?

* What does Scripture mean when it talks about the eyes of the Lord being upon you?

  Read 2 Chronicles 16:9

* We are forever in His sight if we turn and look for Him. What does it mean to turn away from yourself (repent)?

Chapter 15

Bear Hunting Tests Our Faith

The Faithfulness of God

The numerous unpopulated forests of the inland Northwest states provide excellent habitat for large black bear populations. When my good friend, nationally acclaimed artist Max Griener, thought about adding to his collection of big game animals taken with his bow, the elusive black bear was foremost in his mind.

While Max prefers to use a spot-and-stalk method to take game, many hunters find the use of dogs or baited areas a real advantage in locating an animal quickly.

Hunting bear in heavily baited areas can be a challenge. Legal hunting time is during daylight hours, and the black bear is primarily a nocturnal animal. This means that the best time to locate the animal is after dark. This, coupled with the fact that a bear might only rarely visit a particular baited area, produces a challenging scenario for any hunter.

Most often a good guide will set out several baits where considerable sign has been seen. The hunter can either sit in a nearby stand, where he can direct his attention to one particular bait, or use dogs to help check for sign in several areas.

Dogs tend to run down game and tree the critters, allowing the hunter an easy twenty-yard shot. After locating game the insistent barking and howling of the dogs precisely direct the hunters to their quarry.

In the early fall of 1976, Max Griener joined six friends near McCall, Idaho, to bowhunt for elk and bear with guide Ray Rawls. Max felt inclined to patiently try his luck from a tree stand waiting for a bear to appear. "I sat patiently for six days, from daylight until dark, thirteen hours a day, over a pile of rotting meat waste. By the end of the week, I had yet to see my first bear, even though a big bear had been coming into my bait every other night."

After spending hours photographing the bear's tracks, its droppings and the empty meat buckets, Max was frustrated, but he was affirmed in his convictions that his stand would have an eventual payoff. The other hunters had fared well: two bears taken with dogs and a nice six-point bull elk harvested with a bow.

On the last evening, Max listened to the celebration of the successful hunters and thought about his destiny. As the evening passed, celebratory conversation turned to serious discussions about the power of God over creation and the importance of faith. A few companions had not yet accepted Christ as their Lord and Savior. Max's testimony was bold and challenging to those still searching for God's purpose in their lives.

Some of the discussion centered upon whether God was still in the miracle business. Much like the New Testament disciples, these modern-day hunters needed some confirmation of God's presence.

The room emptied as Max sat alone reflecting upon the promises of God's Word. "It was just after the guys went to bed that a thought flashed into my mind. The strong impression that overwhelmed me was that I would kill a bear the next morning; it would be the bear I had been hunting all week; it would be at my bait; I would kill the bear with a single arrow, and it would die instantly."

Max recalled the detail of his vision and yet knew beyond a doubt that without faith and perseverance this prophecy would not be fulfilled. "I was so totally sure that God had spoken to me, I told everyone at breakfast the next morning of my anticipated hunt."

The guide told Max and the other hunters that all the baits had been hit at least two or three times during the week and the probability that a particular bear would be on Max's bait was really slim. Since Max's stand was farthest out, it would be checked after all twenty other baited areas could be analyzed. The group was curious and decided to follow Max and the guide as they visited the baits.

By mid-morning all the baits had been checked, except for two. Unbelievably, not one single bait had been hit overnight by a bear. "I remember Ray asking me which of the two remaining baits I thought we should check first. My answer was that it didn't make any difference; the bear was at my bait."

By this time the hunters and guides were beginning to get hysterical. They could not believe the faith Max displayed in God delivering his bear. Max continued to remain confident and calm that everything God had revealed to him was coming to pass. And it was coming to pass in front of nine witnesses who heard his prediction and had laughed only minutes earlier.

As they approached the last bait, the dogs went wild. Examination of the fresh tracks revealed that the bear Max had been hunting all week had recently visited the bait. The chase began, with dogs and people running everywhere. The dogs looked up and started yelping. Just a few yards from Max's stand was a giant spruce tree with a 350-pound angry bear climbing to the top.

Everyone gathered around the tree to get a good camera angle, cautiously admiring the beast. Max wasn't sure how the bear would react to the arrow. It was snarling and growling at all the intruders.

Max briefly thought about his encounter and how it might put himself and his friends in harm's way. It took some faith and courage to act upon the promise that he had received only hours before.

Everyone was a bit uneasy waiting for Max to nock his first arrow. The adrenaline was rushing through his body as he pulled back the stiff limbs for his shot. The release was flawed, with a quick peak, and the arrow hit a nearby limb. Knowing its fate, the bear hunkered down so only a ten-inch portion of its chest remained visible. As Max peered through his peep sight, the thirty-five-yard shot seemed like a mile. He again drew back his sixty-seven-pound bow and released another arrow only to miss again.

His next four arrows also missed. With only two arrows remaining, Max dejectedly reached for an arrow when one of his friends said, "Max, everything you told us has come true so far. Remember, you said that your promise was you would kill the bear with one arrow: you didn't say anything about how many arrows you would have to shoot!"

With increased faith and confidence in what God had promised, Max pulled back once again and released the string. True to its prophecy and purpose, the arrow found its mark. It penetrated the lungs and heart, lodging the broadhead in the spine of the old bear. The critter was dead before it hit the ground. Everyone stood in amazement at the events that had taken place. A miracle of faith had been experienced by all.

Power Comes From Faith

The Christian life is "a land of hills and valleys" (Deuteronomy 11:11 NASB). In one day, a person can move from the assurance of glory to the attacks of a doubting spirit. It is when our faith is strong that we reap the benefits of a close walk with the Almighty. We can sense His character and feel His presence.

The prophet Isaiah reminds us that our power and performance are directly related to our trust in God. "Kings will see you and rise up, princes will see and bow down, because of the LORD, who is faithful, the Holy One of Israel, who has chosen you" (Isaiah 49:7).

The apostle Paul adds: "God, who has called you into fellowship with his Son Jesus Christ our Lord, is faithful" (1 Corinthians 1:9).

You ask, "How do I know I can trust God? Just because some prophet told us God is faithful doesn't make it so." And then there are those who would ask, "Where do you get such faith?"

Most people like knowing that they aren't the first to try something. Isn't it great that God carefully recorded and documented a list of people who testify to His faithfulness? I encourage you to open your Bible and read Hebrews 11, a roundup of Bible figures whose faith was rewarded by God's faithfulness.

Faith Is Our Foundation

From the beginning of time, God has asked mankind to believe in Him. There is nothing more essential to Christians than their faith. Look up the word "faith" in a good Bible concordance and you will see more than 300 references in the Old and New Testaments.

Faith requires an unquestioning belief in God that does not require proof or evidence. Jesus regularly reminded His disciples, "Have faith in God" (Mark 11:22).

Faith is believing. Believing in the object of our trust—God Almighty. Ed Hindson introduces us to a number of intriguing concepts about faith in his book *Men of the Promise*. In the very first chapter Ed suggests the following:

> *The power of our faith rests in the object of our faith. At the foundation of all love is a belief in the object that is loved. If I do not believe in a person, I cannot love him. The same is true in our relationship with God. Without faith it is impossible for us to know Him and love Him. Faith is the starting point in our spiritual journey. We must begin with God: believing that He exists, believing that He cares, and believing that His love is real.*[1]

Our model of faith comes from studying the character of God. We understand that if God is self-existent, He must be self-sufficient, and if He has power to rule, He must have power over all creation.

And if He is unchanging, He must be faithful. To change would be to become unfaithful.

As A.W. Tozer explains, "God, being who He is, cannot cease to be what He is, and being what He is, He cannot act out of character with Himself. He is at once faithful and unchanging, so all His words and acts must be and must remain faithful."[2]

When you think about it, we have faith in a lot of things. Faith the sun will come up in the morning. Faith that there will be seasons. Faith in the miracle of birth. Faith in the feeling of love. Why not faith in the God who created it all?

The Rock of Our Salvation

The apostle Paul suggests, "We live by faith, not by sight" (2 Corinthians 5:7). I have found it very helpful in growing my faith to keep a little journal in the front part of my Bible. I write down all the answers to prayer as a reminder of God's faithfulness. It is easy to forget how faithful God has been unless we regularly review His accomplishments. Knowing of His past works will help us trust and obey His commands and promises in the future. The book of Hebrews presents evidence for all generations to see that we worship and serve a faithful God.

Eugene Peterson has developed a unique modern-day paraphrase of the New Testament called *The Message*. It helps us better understand the truths that help transform our unbelieving lives into faith-filled lives of commitment.

Here is Peterson's interpretation of Hebrews 11:1: "The fundamental fact of existence is that this trust in God, this faith, is the firm foundation under everything that makes life worth living. It's our handle on what we can't see. The act of faith is what distinguished our ancestors, set them above the crowd. By faith, we see the world called into existence by God's word, what we see created by what we don't see."[3]

A Bear Delivered by Faith

In our daily living we are encouraged to live by faith (see Romans 1:17). The byproduct of a faith-filled life is joy (see Acts 16:34), peace (Romans 15:13), confidence (Isaiah 28:16), and much hope (Romans 5:2).

The authority over our circumstances is directly related to the faith we have. Our faith grows as we exercise through spiritual discipline and devotion. It is our faith in God that brings Him glory (see Romans 4:20).

As we contemplate the faith Max demonstrated in taking his 350-pound trophy black bear, I can think of three lessons we can use to help strengthen our faith.

- **Faith is the ability to leave unfinished work in the hands of God.** As the author of Hebrews reminds us, faith means being sure of the things we hope for while trusting God's will for the results. Not every hunter who has strong faith will bag a bear.

But knowing that we serve a faithful God who enjoys blessing His children helps us understand that He will give us what is appropriate for the occasion. God will use His wonderful riches in Christ Jesus to give us everything we need (see Philippians 4:19).

- **Faith is most powerful during frightening times.** Once again, we can think of all the Old and New Testament saints who, with an abiding faith, battled through tremendous challenges to see victory. Even though we may be tested by fire, our faith will result in His praise, glory, and honor. We may have affliction, lose our job, have a flood take away our home, or experience the death of a loved one, but if we have an abiding faith we know that the ultimate, eternal picture is one that God has painted.

  Chuck Swindoll has said, "Nothing touches you that hasn't first passed through the loving hands of God." If we really believe that God has our best interest at hand, then these temporal problems will take their proper place on the eternal timeline.

- **Faith includes the confidence that God hears and answers our prayers.** With the same faith that led Max to that bear and encouraged him to fire one more arrow, we see the practical blessings God provided. What simple request is God making of you? The apostle James tells us that faith without deeds (some positive efforts on your part) is dead (James 2:26). Jesus told the crippled man who had been lowered into a hut from the roof by a few friends to pick up his bed and walk. The act of faith by the man was to first pick up his bed (see Mark 2:5-12).

Friend, Jesus is asking you to nock an arrow of commitment so that you can make the shot of faith into an eternal relationship with the living God. Do it today! A special prize is awaiting you!

In Paul's letters to the Galatians, he compares the foolishness of the law with the promises that faith holds. His basic message is that we are free in Christ and are no longer bond-servants to the laws, traditions, or personal preferences of others. Because of our maturing faith, we can experience the freedom of our salvation. If we are to be truly committed and righteous before God, we must have great faith.

How Does God Want to Bless You?

God wants to see His children blessed and encouraged. Through a personal relationship with each person, God will reveal His plan and purpose for our lives.

You ask, "How can I take that first step of faith to receive Him as my Lord and Savior?" Scripture suggests that we trust in Him by doing the following:

1. Admit to God that you are a sinner and are in need of a Savior.

2. Be willing to repent (turn away from) your sins.

3. Believe that Jesus Christ died for you on the cross and rose bodily from the grave.

4. By prayer, invite Jesus Christ to come in and take control of your life through the Holy Spirit.

5. Get into a "fishermen's fellowship" (a church).

6. Acknowledge your decision publicly. Tell others of your new found faith.

7. Write to me so I can support you with prayer and resources.

Personal Application

- Job is an example of a person whose faith was really tested. His obedience and loyalty were strong. What is it about Job's life that you would like to assimilate in your life?

  Read Job

- Do you desire to please God? Your faith and obedience are key to experiencing His presence.

  Read Mark 11

Chapter 16

On the Right Track

Finding God

I generally tell folks that releasing an arrow or pulling a trigger is the dividend a hunter receives if he has paid the price of being persistent. Becoming an accomplished woodsman requires a special dedication to pursuing an elusive goal.

Properly tracking a wild creature involves countless hours of evaluation and exploration. You need to be part scientist, part private investigator, part native guide and part conservationist to be a good tracker. Each time a hunter goes into the woods is a time to look for new clues that will help him adapt to his skills.

Not all hunts end with an animal on the ground. There are many others ways to gauge a successful hunt. The appreciation for the adventure and the knowledge gained through viewing nature from the animal's perspective all contribute to a good day in the woods.

I recall an elk-hunting trip in Idaho when days of investigation allowed us the opportunity to locate a herd of elk. It was unfortunate that about the time we were closing in on these critters a severe windstorm—and firestorm—chased us out of the woods.

Early into the trip I noticed that most hunters were driving on Forest Service roads looking for an animal that might stumble into an area adjoining a road for an easy shot. Our group set out to explore remote game trails and meadow areas for fresh sign.

We were hunting in the second week of the season and observing that hunting pressure was pretty intense. You could tell that the animals were frightened and confused as they modified their behavior to accommodate man's intrusion into their habitat. Most hunters sought out the more predictable wallows, ponds, and meadows to seek their prey. Our group was different.

My two hunting partners and I found fresh sign and followed it away from the established roadways and campsites. By following tracks and fresh sign, we came upon some lingering cow elk and elected not to take them. The fresh sign of bulls was all around us as we continued to investigate these new areas.

As we looked to the ground and surrounding vegetation to survey its evidence, the intensity of the windstorm was increasing with every minute. It was while sitting under a large tree during the windstorm that I paused to reflect upon the enormity of God's great creation. It was then that I really appreciated the numerous signs God has given us to identify His presence in nature.

The squirrels were busy chattering away and preparing their food supplies for the winter. The birds were actively reinforcing their nests to withstand the stress of the coming storm. The hawks and eagles circled high above, occasionally squawking out calls of warning to all who would listen. Mr. Black Bear was chowing down on all the berries and roots he could find to prepare for the long winter ahead.

God had given me the privilege of a front-row seat to His majestic creation and its preparation for the pending tempest. The creatures knew before our most reliable weatherman that something major was about to happen. The intensity of the animal activity grew to a climax just before the storm hit our area. I remember how awestruck I was by the movements and preparations of the animals. A thoughtful observer to this event would see that each critter telegraphed its intentions with its actions, attitudes, and behaviors. And as part of their work, wherever the animals contacted the environment they left their calling cards, or sign.

The experience in the northern Idaho woods taught me a lot about how to find game.

I concluded there are two ways to find game. You can stumble around in the woods hoping your path will cross an unsuspecting beast, or you can begin to study the animals and their habitat so that your efforts become more directed. Finding game depends more on understanding their habits, environs, behavioral patterns, and movements than on following consecutive hoofmarks on a trail.

A good hunter will spend up to eighty percent of his time scouting and researching before he actually enters into the stalk or hunt. It is important to remember that consistent hunting success happens through discipline and practice and is not based upon magic or luck.

Before we discuss specific tracking techniques, it is helpful to have a common understanding of the habits and movements of big game animals.

Patterns of Movement

Generally game are found at higher elevations in the summer than in late fall or winter. Game will frequent the higher elevations during the hotter times of the year to escape insects, heat, and high-traffic areas. Food source is always key.

Once the winter storms begin, most game migrate to lower elevations seeking out quiet clearings and new food sources. Larger male animals will hang out in the upper peripheries of a specific area. As a big bass likes the security of being near the deepest water, big bulls and bucks like the protection of steeper terrain. The biggest males ordinarily will follow the females and smaller animals into and out of areas, almost always taking a cautious and deliberate route.

Most game feed in early morning hours and again at dusk, bedding down, shading up, or moving to slightly higher elevations during midday. Creeks and streams, found at lower elevations, provide needed water. It is common to see game feeding in more open areas as their resting partners cuddle up in nearby protected spots.

By following the air currents, game can smell their way to safety. As the day warms up, air currents move up the hill, gorge, or slope. Conversely, in the cool of the evening, the wind currents usually move downhill. A discerning animal will take advantage of this phenomenon by "scenting out" trouble long before it stumbles upon it.

Much like the big bass, most game like edges. They tend to drift into and out of the dense vegetation from meadow areas and clearings. Browsers and grazers like to feed on vegetation that requires more sunlight, but the heavier-forested area provide protective concealment from predators.

Game will often move along the edge just inside the heavy cover. Game will tend to concentrate during severe storms while moving toward open areas during clearing, colder weather.

In a similar manner, game that are pressured by predators or human intervention will scatter. Unmolested game will follow their normal predictable behaviors.

Finding Game

Wild game are no different from humans. They have their daily routines and bodily functions. They must eat, excrete, rest, reproduce, avoid conflict, fellowship, and select comfortable habitat.

Successful hunters know the importance of looking for "the sign." When you are trying to locate a critter, it makes a big difference if you can find sign that tells you about the animal's habits and location. If you know how to read the sign well, you might even get a good idea of how long it has been since the animal was in that area.

A friend of mine once said, "Animals don't wear diapers or eat at McDonald's." But even though animals don't throw away trash, they do leave evidence of their presence. Wherever an animal walks, sleeps, feeds, mates, or plays, it will leave tell-tale signs. A discerning hunter can use these signs to learn about the animal, judge its size and sex, and predict its behavior.

Sign takes many forms. It may be a strong, heavy track; a matted, weedy area that was used as a bed; a thrashed tree used for rubbing the velvet off antlers; cool, moist areas that the animal rolled in (wallow); broken twigs or brush that define a path; or droppings and traces of urine that indicate what type of diet they have.

By analyzing these markers you can concentrate your hunting and stalking time on the most productive areas. As an example, a good hunter will follow a set of prints until he can find a place where urine flows and droppings are found. If the urine flow is forward of and between the back hoof marks, the animal he is following is a male. If the flow is behind the back prints, then he is following a female. If the droppings are glazed or warm, the animal is not far ahead. Conversely, if the droppings are dry, flaky and cold, the hunter is on an old trail.

The size of the hoof prints is also important. As a general rule, the bigger the print, the bigger the animal. Several small prints scattered around mid-size prints usually indicate a female with her young.

Following a trail to eating areas will help you determine the most preferred foods. By focusing your hunting and stalking time on forage areas, you can significantly increase your odds of finding animals.

The Master Tracker

Just as a good hunter learns to read sign in order to tell where an animal has been and where he is going, so our Creator has also given us "sign" that we might track our way in developing an eternal relationship. If we are to really know Him, we must follow the sign He has left. After all, He is the Master Tracker and has deliberately set a path to our hearts and minds.

From the beginning of time God has desired to have a meaningful relationship with His creation. Because of Adam and Eve's fall from grace, sin kept them from enjoying a direct relationship with God the Father.

Through direct revelation God inspired and guided a few men and women to record evidence that, when identified and observed, would lead a person to a successful spiritual hunt.

In Old Testament times, God used patriarchs like Moses and Joshua to enlighten His chosen people and explain the mighty miracles they observed. Unfortunately, people thought they had a better plan and disobeyed these messengers. God hoped that people would listen to priests and judges who would rule over the blessed ones. Once again, folks allowed their wills and negative attitudes to guide them. The people complained and argued with God that they needed kings and prophets to help them discern God's will. But even with divinely appointed leaders, the people's desire to be disobedient prevailed.

The triune God realized that a sacrifice was needed in order to receive complete forgiveness and a restored relationship. In previous encounters with various leaders, God had taught that there must be some sort of sacrificial offering made to Him when sin was involved. Recognizing that man's sinful acts had permeated the world, God directed that there must be an ultimate sacrifice for fellowship between Him and His creation to be restored.

God had provided all sorts of signs for those diligently seeking to find Him. Through His laws (including the Ten Commandments) and guidance, He endeavored to direct folks along the trail of restoration. Unfortunately, mankind's own passion and sinful nature blinded the people hunting for a relationship with God.

So God laid another trail for mankind to follow. This trail of evidence leads to a time when God became a human being of flesh and blood in order to free mankind from the bondage of his sinful life. The prophets listened to and recorded God's word as He set forth specific signs that pointed the way to the life and ministry of the God-Man, Jesus Christ.

According to most theologians there are more than 300 direct and specific prophecies (signs) leading to the birth of Christ. Can you imagine having a trail with that many signs on it? We would agree that there is no way you could miss spotting the reward at the end of the trail. Yet despite all the evidence of Christ's coming and the previous miracles to His chosen people, folks turned their attention elsewhere.

Through the miraculous birth of a little Child in a manger, God entered the world so that He could be sacrificed on Calvary's cross for the sinful acts of all mankind. By not following His sign, most people will still fail to see the day of destiny and judgment.

The Trail to Glory

Are you able to trust the guide? Why? Do you know if he has ever been wrong? Has he ever gotten lost or provided bad advice?

If you can't trust your guide all the time, why should you trust the signs of Old Testament prophets? After all, a lot of people claim to be prophets but fail to have 100-percent performance. In Old Testament times, if you failed even once in your prophecy, you would be stoned to death. Fortunately for modern-day hunting guides, their clients do not utilize the same standard to judge a pathfinder's performance!

Moses anticipated a problem with his followers: How would the Israelites know whether a prophet who claimed to speak God's message was a true prophet? (This question is still being asked today.) Then Moses gave the true test of a prophet: "When a prophet speaks in the name of the LORD, if the thing does not come about or come true, that is the thing which the LORD has not spoken" (Deuteronomy 18:22 NASB).

We can now see that the prophetic signs or markers left by biblical ancestors were indeed 100-percent accurate. As we identified some of the signs animals can leave, let's look at just a few of the markers that lead us to pursue a deeper relationship with God. With a history book in one hand and a newspaper in the other, check out the sign along the biblical trail!

Checking the Sign

From the fall of Jerusalem (Jeremiah 25:9-11), to the rebuilding of the Temple (Ezra 3:1-13), to the birth and death of Christ (Isaaiah 7:14; Luke 2:4-11; Matthew 27:33-50) we can see the hand of God marking a spiritual trail for mankind to follow.

Jesus was the fulfillment of virtually hundreds of messianic prophecies in the Old Testament. These include prophecies Jesus couldn't possibly have conspired to fulfill, such as the location of His birthplace (Micah 5:2), being born of a virgin (Isaiah 7:14), and the identity of His forerunner, John the Baptist (Malachi 3:1). There were hundreds of Old Testament prophecies related to Christ's first coming (all of which were literally fulfilled), and there are more than 500 relating to His second coming (see Acts 1:10,11).

We now have arrived at a point on the trail where fresh sign is before us. We are closing in on the target (a deeper understanding of biblical prophecy as related to God's plan for mankind). The new sign continues in the same direction as past markers. Tighten up your spiritual hiking shoes and let's review what is before us.

Future Signs

There is no better way to describe what signs and timing exist on the pathway to the "end times" than to review the words of the God-Man, Jesus. He wanted His followers to know what to expect. With a modern-day translation of God's Word, read Matthew 24 in total for a greater understanding of the signs and markers yet to come.

> Jesus told them, "Don't let anyone fool you. For many will come claiming to be the Messiah and will lead many astray. When you hear of wars beginning, this does not signal my return; these must come, but the end is not yet. The nations and kingdoms of the earth will rise against each other, and there will be famines and earthquakes in many places. But all this will be only the beginning of the horrors to come.

> "Then you will be tortured and killed and hated all over the world because you are mine, and many of you shall fall back into sin and betray and hate each other. And many false prophets will appear and lead many astray. Sin will be rampant everywhere and will cool the love of many. But those enduring to the end shall be saved.

> And the Good News about the Kingdom will be
> preached throughout the whole world, so that
> all nations will hear it, and then, finally, the end
> will come."
>
> —Matthew 24:4-14 (TLB)

With God, as with hunting, we need to periodically stop and analyze the terrain and the evidence if we are to really understand what we are seeing.

The End of the Trail

As a good archer makes his final stalk to a great bull elk, the world scene is set for the final shot. The signs are right, the wind direction is favorable, the bow is poised, and the arrow is nocked.

In a similar manner the Middle East today occupies the attention of world leaders, as it is a focal point of political and social unrest. Those who control the major oil reserves have their grip on the world economy. The European market has new alliances that match prophetic teaching. Apostasy (deserters of the faith) and open denial of biblical truth are evident in the church. Moral chaos becomes more and more evident because of the complete departure from Christian morality. The sweep of spiritism, the occult, and demon worship begin to prepare the world for Satan's final hour. This activity coupled with the moral decay and the universal denigration of the family, suggests that the archer is reaching for the string, the shot is about to be taken.

Are you prepared for the final push up the trail and the end results? For those who want to have a personal relationship with the living God and who want eternal life, the trailhead is the cross. Accepting the 300-plus prophetic utterances that Christ was indeed the Messiah who came to forgive you of your sins is validation enough for this hunter that I'm on the right path! What does the sign mean to you? Don't wait for the trail to grow cold or run out! Accept Christ TODAY!

Remember, once we find God the hunt isn't over. The Holy Spirit will continue to help you hunt for grace, mercy, forgiveness, love, peace, comfort, and joy. It is a lifelong trail of discovering how great a God we serve.

Personal Application

- Why is sign so important to a game hunter and to a Christian? Jesus was the fulfillment of hundreds of prophecies. Why were these so critical?

    Read Micah 5:2; Isaiah 7:14; Malachi 3:1

- Was Jesus really God? What is the evidence of His deity?

    Read about Jesus' works (John 4:54; 6:14; 9:16), Jesus' control of nature (Colossians 1:16; John 2:1-11; John 6:1-15; John 6:16-21), Jesus' healings (Isaiah 35:5,6; John 5:1-15), Jesus' raising people from the dead (John 11:43,44), Jesus' death on the cross (Matthew 27:26-50), and Jesus' resurrection (Luke 24:3; John 20:20; Luke 24:41-43)

Last Shot

Hunting has been defined as hours and hours of sweet anticipation and patient investigation graced by moments of incredible excitement. Whether you journey to the woods with a gun, pistol, muzzle loader, bow, or camera, you will experience a serenity, a beauty and a challenge that will test your hunting skills and character. Qualities like patience, perseverance, self-discipline, commitment and confidence will be strengthened as you deal with each adventure.

It is my prayer that, through the reading of this book you gained a greater awareness of the presence of God in your daily living. Hopefully you now better understand His diverse character through exploring some of His many traits. We have learned that God is the Father of creation and is most gracious, good, merciful, powerful, comforting, just, faithful, and full of love. The great Jehovah is all-powerful and ever present to those who seek Him. It is my hope that as you continue living an abundant life, you will personalize all the unique items (traits) we discovered about God. Your "spiritual pack" is now equipped with meaningful resources that will enable you to have a more productive and joy-filled life.

To the Bible scholars who might wish to analyze this work as being incomplete because not all of God's attributes were thoroughly discussed, I leave with you a quote from my guide on this journey, A. W. Tozer:

> *There is today no lack of Bible teachers to set forth correctly the principles of the doctrines of Christ, but too many of these people seem satisfied to teach the fundamentals of faith year after year, strangely unaware that there is in their ministry no manifest Presence, nor anything unusual in their personal lives. They minister constantly to believers who feel within their breasts a longing which their teaching simply does not*

*satisfy..... It is not mere words that nourish the soul,
but God Himself, and unless and until the hearers find
God in personal experience they are not the better for
having heard the truth."* [1]

Every man lives by faith—the unbelieving person and also
the believer. The unbeliever worships the natural laws of the
universe, while the believer worships the God of all creation.
As an example, when a believer considers the unique
breeding cycles of an elk, he realizes that only a God of order
could have developed such a unique cycle. The cow elk will
be ready to breed at three specific times, each for a nine-hour
period, during the season. The same awesome complexity and
distinctive characteristics God has provided to properly control elk populations are seen throughout His creation. To a
believer this is a wonder and mystery that only a calculating
and caring God could have provided. The unbeliever arrives
at his understanding of this event by a process of reasoning
confirmed by a faith in the philosophy of science. A believer
uses the discoveries of science to help him better understand
teachings of God's Word. The unbeliever assumes that when
all the atoms randomly came together, life was formed and
eventually took shape as man, elk, and other animals.

The Doctrine of the Holy Trinity

God's Word is to be understood because of the accuracy
and truth it provides. In His Word we see clear evidence of the
plurality of God. We can see Him as Father, Son and Holy
Ghost. Jesus testified, "I and my Father are one." When con-
fronted by the Sanhedrin as to His deity, Jesus did not deny
that He was God.

Throughout the gospel of John we see numerous examples of the God-Man, Jesus. The Son of God, testified about His
relationship to the Father through evidence of Scripture, the
testimony of His miracles, the power of His words, and the

character of His person. The people who knew Him best, His family and disciples, often stated, "Truly You are the Son of God" (Matthew 14:33 NKJV).

Knowing that mankind needed a Comforter and Encourager, Jesus promised to leave His Spirit with us in the form of the Holy Spirit.

"And I will ask the Father, and He will give you another Helper, that He may be with you forever" (John 14:16 NASB).

"But the Helper, the Holy Spirit, whom the Father will send in My name, He will teach you all things, and bring to your remembrance all that I said to you" (John 14:26 NASB).

"When the Helper comes, whom I will send to you from the Father, that is the Spirit of truth, who proceeds from the Father, He will bear witness of Me" (John 15:26 NASB).

In a mystical way, beyond human comprehension, God is triune (three Persons in one). A simple illustration to help us understand how that is possible comes from viewing a typical mountain-hunting scene from the valley floor. We can see the beautiful snow-capped glaciers resting on the mountaintops. These solid masses of snow and ice will soon begin to melt into a liquid state we know as water. After reaching the valley floor these streams and ponds will begin to evaporate under the heat of day, becoming a vapor. Each state has its own identity, but in whatever form it takes, the substance has the same essential properties. Water is water, and God is God. Whether we experience Him as the Father, the Son or the Holy Spirit.

"The Persons of the Godhead, being one, have one will. They work always together, and never one without the instant acquiescence of the other two does one smallest act. Every act of God is accomplished by the Trinity in Unity." [2]

The real question is: What are you doing with the knowledge you have? If you desire a personal relationship with the living God, if you wish to know Jesus Christ as your personal Savior, if you want the daily comfort of the Holy Spirit, then all you have to do is ask God into your heart (see chapter 15).

Much like the prophet Jeremiah, through God's strength I endeavor to be strong and courageous (see Jeremiah 1:18; 15:20). As in Jeremiah's day, the doom of our nation is being sealed with immorality, ungodly pursuits, idolatry, irreverence for God's favor in government, and disintegration of Christian family values. Without God's mercy and a repentant heart among many, our families and nation will fall, as did Judah.

But God's judgment of His people (and the nation) in Jeremiah's day, though terrible, was not to be the last word, the final work of God in history. His mercy and the repentant hearts of the people would eventually triumph over evil. There was, and will be, restoration and renewal for all who believe.

Through the challenging times, God will ready those who are faithful for service. He will call out disciples to become hunters as He did almost 2,600 years ago: " 'Behold, I am going to send for many fishermen,' declares the LORD, 'and they will fish for them [the lost]; and afterwards I shall send for many hunters, and they will hunt them [the lost] from every mountain and every hill, and from the clefts of the rocks' " (Jeremiah 16:16 NASB).

I share with you openly that this study for me is only the beginning of really knowing God. To really be acquainted with God, we must daily study and fellowship with Him. Our love for our heavenly Father needs to grow through a discipled prayer life and Bible study.

One of my favorite authors is David C. Needham. In his great work *Close to His Majesty,* he encourages us to become more intimate with the Father: "It is easy to forget that God saved us above all else for love, for intimacy in relationship, for response. To fail to have time for this is to fail at living. Certainly His intentions are that everything else—service, witnessing, practical holiness—be a byproduct of our love for Him." [3]

It is your turn, my friend. God is calling upon you to hunt for others and to share His message of hope, joy, peace, love, and grace. String up your spiritual bow, sharpen the arrows of truth, take steady aim on those who don't know God, and begin to graciously teach and encourage all who wish to know the God of all creation (see Matthew 28:18-20). Good hunting!

For the Lighthearted
Humorous Tales

"That's My Deer"

I'm reminded of a story about two friends from a little rural church. Buck had been an avid outdoorsman for years. Lance was an executive with a major company and an Ivy League college graduate. While he was skilled in many facets of life, he had no clue about getting along in the outdoors.

The two men met at a men's fellowship gathering when Buck decided to ask Lance along on a hunting trip. The elk were in the rut, and opening day was fast approaching.

As dawn was breaking, Buck and Lance broke camp and started heading out to the hilly terrain. Buck suggested that the two separate to cover more area.

"Lance, you head over to that ridgeline and keep a good eye on the valley below. I'll head out over to the hill across from you. If you get in trouble or shoot an elk, just fire three shots in the air and I'll come runnin'."

About thirty minutes had passed when Buck heard a single shot and then three rapid shots. Buck was excited as he recognized the agreed-upon signal. "Cool, his first time in the woods and he already got an elk," he said.

Buck moved quickly towards Lance's position. As he crossed a small hill, he could see Lance in a clearing holding off another man with his gun.

Buck gingerly walked up to Lance, who was yelling at the man, "That is my elk, and you can't have it." The man looked at Buck with a confused expression and said, "Okay, okay, mister. You win. You can have your elk—if you will just let me take my saddle off him."

Dog Days and Goose Hunting

City slickers Bill and Joe were not the brightest individuals. In fact, they were about as bright as an Alaskan December. It seems that these two buddies had never gone duck hunting before and set out to break a record for the most birds in one day. They bought two beautiful guns, several boxes of shells, decoys, camouflage gear and a good hunting dog.

They hunted through the morning on into the late afternoon without a single bird. Finally, Bill said to Joe, "Maybe we'd do better if we threw our dog up higher."

A Good Shot

A guy from Oklahoma was hunting in Colorado when the game warden approached his camp. He noticed a nice-looking deer hung proudly in the corner of camp. As he inspected the deer, he noticed that the animal had been shot right between the eyes. The warden asked the hunter if he considered himself a good shot."

The hunter replied, "Of course. All outdoorsmen from Oklahoma are good shots."

The next day the warden came by the same camp only to see a nice six-by-six elk hanging on the tree next to the buck. He inspected the animal to once again discover that this hunter had shot the animal right between the eyes.

"Good shot!" the warden exclaimed.

The warden continued to look with amazement at the animals as he said to the hunter, "I have a bear tag that hasn't been used. Do you suppose you can get me a nice black bear?"

"No problem," remarked the hunter.

Sure enough, the next day the warden came by to see a beautiful six-foot black bear hanging next to the other two animals.

The warden noticed the bear had been shot through both paws and between his eyes. With puzzlement written all over his face, the warden asked the hunter, "How did the bear get three wounds?"

The hunter replied, "When the bright light from my 1 million-candlepower spotlight hit his eyes, he covered his face with his paws and I shot."

Football Players Get Revenge?

My friend Brent Jones, former All Pro tightend with the San Francisco 49ers, tells a great story about two hunters. Brent, Dave Dalby (center) and Harris Barton (All Pro guard) were heading up to a private duck pond in northern California. The boys were recovering from a very difficult defeat the day before. Everyone was in a bad mood.

Leaving his teammates in the truck, Brent went up to the old farmhouse to check in with the property owner to make sure it was all right for them to proceed with their trip.

Brent asked the farmer for permission to hunt his ponds.

The farmer said, "Sure, you can hunt the ponds, but would you do me a favor?"

Brent was only too willing to assist the farmer.

"You see, my old mule has cancer and I can't bring myself to shoot her. She really needs to be put out of her misery. Could you handle that?"

As Brent was walking back to the truck, he decided to play a trick on his friends. He briskly approached the truck and slammed the door.

With alarm written on their tired faces, his buddies looked at Brent and asked, "Did he give you permission?"

Brent grumbled, "No way—the guy's a real grouch."

Brent jumped out of the truck, grabbed his 12-gauge shotgun and some shells, and proceeded to the corral in front of the truck as he shouted out, "I'll show him!"

Brent walked up to the ol' mule and fired away.

No sooner had the mule hit the deck when Brent heard several shots coming from the back of the truck. Brent looked over at Dave and Harris, who had just shot the farmer's prized colts. Harris yelled out, "I guess we showed him! Let's get out of here!"

A Loaded Gun and Wild Bird

A Potosi, Missouri, newspaper reported the following occurrence: "A man showing off a turkey he thought he had killed was shot in the leg last week when the wounded bird thrashed around in his car trunk and triggered his shotgun.

" 'The turkeys are fighting back' said Sheriff Ron Skiles.' And well they might; it turns out that Larry Lands, who was in satisfactory condition in the hospital in Potosi, and his son Larry Jr., 16, were hunting a week before the start of turkey season and will probably be fined."

Only in Arkansas

"Only in Arkansas" was the headline of this article from the *Arkansas Democrat Gazette:*

"Two local men were seriously injured when their pickup truck left the road and hit a tree near Cotton Plant on State Highway 38 early Monday morning.

"Thurston Poole, 33, of Des Arc, and Billy Ray Wallis, 38, of Little Rock are listed in serious condition at Baptist Medical Center. The accident occurred as the two men were returning to Des Arc after a frog-gigging trip. (Note to city slickers: Frog gigging, or frog sticking, is how, armed with a small pitchfork, you catch frogs from the bayou bank. Frog legs make a tasty supper.)

"On an overcast Sunday night, Poole's pickup truck headlights malfunctioned. The two men concluded that the headlight fuse on the older-model truck was burned out. As a replacement fuse was not available, Wallis noticed that the .22-caliber bullet from his pistol fit perfectly into the fuse box next to the steering wheel column. Upon inserting the bullet, the lights again began to operate and the two men proceeded on east toward the White River Bridge.

"After traveling approximately 25 miles and just before crossing the river, the bullet apparently overheated, discharged and struck Poole in the groin. The vehicle pulled sharply to the right, exiting the pavement and striking a tree. Poole suffered only minor cuts and abrasions from the accident, but will require surgery to repair the other wound. Wallis sustained a broken clavicle and was treated and released.

" 'Thank God we weren't on that bridge when Thurston shot himself or we might have been dead,' said Wallis. 'I've been a trooper for 10 years in this part of the world,' said Deputy Snyder, 'but this is a first for me. I can't believe that those two would admit how the accident happened.'

"Upon being notified of the wreck, Lavinia Poole asked how many frogs the boys had caught, and did anyone think to get them from the truck."

Dynamite and Gun Dogs

Swen and Irving were great hunting and fishing partners. It was late fall, and the ducks were really plentiful in the early morning and late evening. The two outdoorsmen decided to try doing some ice fishing during the afternoon when the shooting action for birds wasn't real good.

They arrived at the shores of the lake to find that the ice was pretty firm and thick. Swen put his new four-by-four in "all 4 low" and charged out on the ice. When the truck stopped the doors sprung open and Irving's big black Lab, Daisy, sprang out. She was a great retriever but was a little stupid.

When you looked at Daisy, you realized the "gates are down, the lights are flashing but the train isn't coming."

The two men began to dig a hole for their ice fishing when they realized that it was considerably deeper than they originally thought. Swen remembered he had some dynamite, from his construction job, in the lock box at the back of his truck.

Using the truck as a barrier, Swen tossed a lit stick of TNT as far as he could. The dynamite hit the area where the shallow hole was dug. With great anticipation the outdoorsmen waited for the explosion.

Well, Daisy wasn't going to wait. She decided that this "stick" needed to be retrieved. Despite the frantic instructions of her master to forget the stick and come back, Daisy picked up the lit TNT and proudly returned it to the truck. The frightening yells of both men caused the dog to cower and duck under the truck. At this point the men took off running as the dynamite blew a large hole in the ice. They are still looking for the truck and Daisy.

Hunters and Their Techniques

Professors of mathematics will prove the existence of at least one unique deer and then leave the detection and harvesting of an actual deer as an exercise for their graduate students.

Economists don't hunt deer, but they believe that if deer are paid enough, they will hunt for themselves.

Statisticians hunt the first animal they see "N" times and call it a deer.

Politicians don't hunt deer, but they will share the deer you shoot with the people who voted for them.

Lawyers also don't hunt deer, but they follow the herds around arguing about who owns the droppings.

Bear Alert

The Sierra Club is advising hikers, hunters, and fishermen to take extra precautions and keep alert for bears while in the field. We advise that outdoorsmen wear noisy little bells on their clothing so as not to startle bears that aren't expecting them. We also advise outdoorsmen to carry pepper spray with them in case of an encounter with a bear.

It is also a good idea to watch out for fresh signs of bear activity. Outdoorsmen should recognize the difference between black bear and grizzly bear scat. Black bear sign is smaller and contains lots of berries and squirrel fur. Grizzly bear sign has little bells in it and smells like pepper.

Glossary of Terms

Deity—The state of being God, His divine nature, the Godhead. Since Jesus' use of the words "I am" (John 6:35,48,51; 8:18,58) echoes the self-affirmation of Yahweh found in Isaiah 43:10 and 48:12, it is likely that we should see them as a veiled indication of the deity of Jesus.

Eternal—God is not bound by time; all things are equally past, present and future to Him.

Glassing—You spend hours looking through binoculars or a gun scope trying to find animals who are neatly camouflaged in the vegetation.

Guide—A local guy with a good knowledge of the woods but a better knowledge of economics. He owns a new truck, a camper and two ATVs with money he acquired from greenhorns (people new to hunting) gullible enough to believe that by running around in the woods looking at deer and bear droppings they will somehow discover the world record animal that has eluded the master-hunters for years.

Holiness—The attribute by which God eternally wills and maintains His own moral excellence, abhors sin, and demands purity of His mortal creatures.

Immutable—God is unchangeable in His person, His will and His purpose

Infinite—God has no limitations.

Information Signs—When you see a road sign that says "Bear left," it doesn't mean the bear relocated.

Omnipotent—God is able to do anything that is consistent with His nature and will. God is the ultimate and absolute cause of all things. He is all-powerful.

Omnipresent—God is not limited by space and is present in every point of space with His whole being. He is transcendent and present at all times.

Omniscient—God has a complete and simultaneous knowledge of all things actual and possible, past, present, and future. God knows all things that exist in actuality.

Sign—Any type of evidence left by the animal (such as droppings, hoof prints, scrape or rub areas, fur left on branches, cast antlers, feeding ground, and bedding areas).

Wallow—An area that is wet or damp where an animal can cool off, comfort himself or relieve himself of pesty bugs. A place where he can roll about, bathe, toss or immerse himself.

Wrangler—An accomplished woodsman or a guy who, like a six-pack of Coke, is missing the plastic thingy to hold it all together.

Notes

Chapter 1
1. Dr. Paul Brand and Philip Yancey, *Fearfully and Wonderfully Made* (Grand Rapids, MI: Zondervan Books, 1987), p. 21.
2. Elmer B. Smick, *Hunting—Baker's Dictionary of Christian Ethics* (Grand Rapids: Baker Publishing, 1973), p. 21, 397

Chapter 2
1. J.D. Douglas, *New Bible Dictionary—Second Edition* (Wheaton, IL: Tyndale House Publishers, Inc., 1984), pp. 428-429.
2. Ibid.

Chapter 3
1. Carroll E. Simcox, *3000 Quotations on Christian Themes,* (Grand Rapids, MI: Baker Book House, 1975), p. 10.

Chapter 4
1. A.W. Tozer, *The Knowledge of the Holy* (New York, NY: Walker and Company, 1996), pp. 175-176.
2. Cynthia Heald, *Becoming a Woman of Grace* (Nashville, TN: Thomas Nelson Publishers, 1998), p. 2.
3. Wayne A. Barber, *The Rest of Grace* (Eugene, OR: Harvest House Publishers, 1998), p. 27.
4. Charles Swindoll, *The Grace Awakening* (Dallas, TX: Word Publishing, 1990), p. 9.
5. Carroll E. Simcox, *3,000 Quotations on Christian Themes* (Grand Rapids, MI: Baker Book House, 1975), p. 134.
6. Donald Grey Barnhouse, *Romans, Man's Ruin,* Vol. 1 (Grand Rapids, MI.: Wm. B. Eerdmans Publishing Company, 1952), p. 72.
7. John Piper, *Future Grace* (Sisters, OR: Multnomah Books, 1995), p. 766.
8. *The Hymnal for Worship and Celebration,* (Waco, TX: Word Music, 1986) #202.

Chapter 5
1. A.W. Tozer, *The Knowledge of the Holy* (New York, NY: Walker and Company, 1996), pp. 171-172.

Chapter 6
1. See the Website for Equipped to Serve at www.equipped.org.
2. Ronald F. Youngblood. General Editor, with F.F. Bruce and R.K. Harrison, Consulting Editors, *Nelson's New Illustrated Bible Dictionary,* (Nashville, TN: Thomas Nelson, 1997).
3. Ibid.
4. James Robison, *Knowing God as Father* (Fort Worth, TX: Life Today, 1996), p. 1.
5. James Robison, *Thank God, I'm Free* (Nashville, TN: Thomas Nelson Publishers, 1988), pp. 19-20.
6. Ibid., pp. 26-27.
7. Robison, *Knowing God As Father*, pp. 14-15.
8. Ibid, pp. 22-23.
9. Ibid.
10. J.D. Douglas, *New Bible Dictionary—Second Edition* (Wheaton, IL: Inter-Tyndale House Publishers, Inc., 1984), pp. 427-429.
11. Robison, *Knowing God As Father,* p. 32.

Chapter 7
1. James Dobson, *Straight Talk to Men and Their Wives* (Carmel, NY: Guideposts, 1980), p. 13.

Chapter 9
1. Charles Stanley, *Dealing with Life's Pressures,* (Atlanta, GA: In Touch Ministries, 1997).

Chapter 10
1. Steve Chapman, *A Look at Life From a Deer Stand* (Eugene, OR: Harvest House Publishers, 1998), p. 15.
2. Carroll E. Simcox, *4400 Quotations for Christian Communicators* (Grand Rapids, MI: Baker Book House, 1991), p. 337.
3. Carroll E. Simcox, *3000 Quotations on Christian Themes,* (Grand Rapids, MI: Baker Book House, 1975), p. 214.
4. Charles Stanley, *Nelson Electronic Bible Reference Library* (Nashville, TN: Nelson Publishing, 1997).
5. John F. MacArthur, *The MacArthur New Testament Commentary* (Chicago, IL: Moody Press, 1983).

Chapter 11
1. David Petersen, *A Hunter's Heart—Honest Essays on Blood Sport* (New York, NY: Henry Holt and Company, 1996), p. 35.
2. Robert A. Gruszecki, *The Wisdom of the Woods* (Calgary, Alberta, Canada: Orion Publications, 1991), pp. 9, 10.

3. Petersen, *A Hunter's Heart*, pp. 37, 38.
4. *Webster's Electronic Dictionary, Fourth Edition*, (Scottsdale, AZ.: Macmillan Publishing, 1999).
5. A. W. Tozer, *The Knowledge of the Holy* (New York, NY: Walker and Company, 1996), p. 154.
6. Charles Stanley, *Eternal Security* (Nashville, TN: Thomas Nelson Publishers, 1997).

Chapter 12

1. Charlie Alsheimer, *Whitetail—Behavior Through the Seasons* (Iola, WI: Krause Publications, 1996), p. 46.
2. Gordon Dahl, *Work, Play and Worship in a Leisure-Oriented Society* (Minneapolis, MN: Augsburg Publishing House, 1972), p. 12.
3. Charles Stanley, *Nelson's Electronic Bible Reference—Listening to God* (Nashville, TN: Thomas Nelson Publishing, 1998).
4. Charles Stanley, *Nelson's Electronic Bible Reference—The Glorious Journey* (Nashville, TN: Thomas Nelson Publishing, 1998).

Chapter 13

1. Robert Gruszecki, *The Wisdom of the Woods* (Orion Publications, Calgary, Alberta, Canada, 1991), p. 6.
2. H. L. Mencken. and Alfred A. Knopf, *A New Dictionary of Quotations* (New York, NY, 1942), pp. 462-463.

Chapter 14

1. John Phillips, *The Masters' Secrets of Deer Hunting* (Lakeland, FL.: Larsen's Outdoor Publishing, 1991).
2. Ronald Youngbloood, *Nelson New Illustrated Bible Dictionary*, (Nashville, TN: Thomas Nelson, 1997).
3. A. W. Tozer, *The Knowledge of the Holy* (New York, NY: Walker and Company, 1996).

Chapter 15

1. Ed Hindson, *Men of the Promise* (Eugene, OR: Harvest House Publishers, 1996), p. 16.
2. A. W. Tozer, *The Knowledge of the Holy* (New York, NY: Walker and Company, 1961), p. 147.
3. Eugene H. Peterson, *The Message* (Colorado Springs, CO: NavPress, 1993), pp. 556-557.

Last Shot
1. A.W.Tozer, *The Pursuit of God* (Camp Hill, PA:Christian Publications, 1982), pp. 8-9.
2. A.W.Tozer, *The Knowledge of the Holy,* (New York, NY:Walker and Company, 1996), pp. 40-41.
3. David C. Needham, *Close to His Majesty* (Portland, OR: Multnomah Press,1987), pp. 13-14.

About the Author

Jim Grassi was born and reared in the San Francisco Bay area. His thirty-three years of professional experience in the outdoors have given him a unique perspective on fishing and hunting. He has harvested several SCI record-book animals and photographed many more. Jim now utilizes a compound bow or digital camcorder for most of his hunting.

He is the founder and president of the culturally strategic Let's Go Fishing Ministries, Inc. Known for his evangelistic heart, he teaches folks from a background as an outdoorsman, professional fisherman, college professor, businessman, community leader, and pastor. Recently Let's Go Fishing Ministries has developed a variety of outreach-oriented materials to help the local church and Christian conference centers reach their communities utilizing an outdoor sports ministry platform. Grassi is a trustee of the Sports Outreach of America, an association united to create greater evangelistic ministry through sports.

Grassi is an award-winning author, communicator, outdoorsman, pastor, and former television co-host. He brings a sense of challenge and excitement to his public presentations. Through his multimedia programs he encourages participants to develop a better understanding and appreciation for God's great outdoors. His practical approach to teaching biblical truth has captivated audiences around the world.

His first three books were best-sellers in the first few weeks. *In Pursuit of the Prize* won the prestigious Silver Angel Award for excellence in media. As a member of the Outdoor Writers Association of America, he has written numerous magazine articles and booklets on hunting and fishing. Grassi has been featured on outdoor television programs and Christian television and radio programs including: *The 700 Club, The Carol Lawrence Show, Cornerstone Television, Southern*

Baptist Television—Cope, Chicago Television 38, The Dick Staub Show, Getting Together, In Fisherman, Jimmy Houston Outdoors, and *Home Life.*

As a popular public speaker, Jim is available for pulpit fill, men's outreach gatherings, Christian conference centers, sportsmen's banquets and evangelism training workshops. He is the 1996 Recipient of the Faith and Freedom Award for the Religious Heritage of America Foundation and has been recognized in the International Who's Who for his work in promoting Christian family values.

Of utmost importance to Jim are his wife of more than thirty-five years, his married twin sons who are pastors, and his three wonderful grandchildren. He now resides in Post Falls, Idaho, along the shores of the beautiful Spokane River. For more information about Let's Go Fishing Ministries or booking Jim as a speaker, please contact: Let's Go Fishing Ministries, P.O. Box 3303, Post Falls, ID 83877 (on the Internet: www.letsgofishing.org).

Other Harvest House Books:
Promising Waters—Stories of Fishing and Following Jesus
Heaven on Earth—True Stories of Fishing and Faith
In Pursuit of the Prize—Finding God in the Great Outdoors

A Personal Message

Dear Friend,

I have been privileged to be involved with outdoor ministries for almost twenty years. Through countless conferences, retreats, family camps, Special Kids Days for the disabled, single-parent programs, men's ministry events, and sportsmen's banquets, I have endeavored to present God's Word in a practical manner. The model I use in shaping my presentations is Jesus. Through the use of anecdotes, metaphors and parables, I utilize real-life stories from my hunting and fishing background and associations to help individuals focus on strengthening families and training disciples.

Let's Go Fishing Ministries is one of the oldest outdoor sports ministries in the country. We have held hundreds of successful family-oriented events that provide recreational skills training while helping to build lifelong memories. Utilizing expert instructors, we encourage and motivate folks to become proficient in hunting, archery, boating, hiking, and, of course, fishing.

LGFM has been a resource organization for churches and national ministries wishing to impact their communities with relevant messages and memory-building experiences. Most recently, we have embarked upon a unique and exciting vision to develop state-of-the-art multimedia presentations to assist others in giving dynamic presentations on various outdoor sports.

These presentations will ultimately be available through the Internet and will provide testimonials and technique presentations from some of the top Christian hunters, fishermen, archers, and outdoorsmen in the world. The detailed format of program development and implementation will assist even the smallest fellowship in presenting a "world-class" program.

These resources are ideal for community outreach events, conference ministry, men's ministry programs, women of the wilderness meetings, youth rallies and pastor retreats.

For more information on how you can access these resources, contact: Jim Grassi, P.O. Box 3303, Post Falls, ID 83877 or through our Website at www.letsgofishing.org.

In His Service,

Jim Grassi

Feel Free to Contact and Support These Outdoor Ministries:

Christian Bowhunters of America
3460 West 13th St.
Cadillac, MI 49601
(616) 775-7744

Christian Deer Hunters Association
P.O. Box 432
Silver Lake, MN 55381
(320) 327-2266

Christian Sportsman's Fellowship
P.O. Box 566547
Atlanta, GA 31156
(800) 705-7892

God's Great Outdoors
8193 Emerick Rd.
West Milton, OH 45383
(937) 698-3656

Let's Go Fishing Family Ministries
P.O. Box 3303
Post Falls, ID 83877
(208) 457-9619

My Father's World Video Ministries
43 Lima Rd.
Geneseo, NY 14454
(716) 243-5263